TREASURY OF PINEAPPLE DESIGNS FOR CROCHETING

Edited by
Linda Macho

Dover Publications, Inc., New York

General Instructions

* (Asterisk) : This symbol indicates that the instructions immediately following are to be repeated the given number of times plus the original.

**Are used in same way for a second set of repeats within one set of directions.

Repeat instructions in parentheses as many times as specified. For example: " (Ch 5, sc in next sc) 5 times" means to work all that is in parentheses 5 times in total.

CROCHET ABBREVIATIONS

ch	Chain
st	Stitch
sl st . . .	Slip st.
s c	Single Crochet
s d c . . .	Short Double Crochet
d c	Double Crochet
tr c . . .	Treble Crochet
d tr c . . .	Double Treble Crochet
tr tr c . . .	Triple Treble Crochet
o m . . .	Open Mesh. Sometimes termed sp-Space
s m . . .	Solid Mesh. Sometimes termed bl-Block
p	Picot
d p . . .	Double Picot
beg. rnd . .	Beginning Round
incl . . .	Inclusive
inc . . .	Increase
dec . . .	Decrease

Published in Canada by General Publishing Company, Ltd., 30 Lesmill Road, Don Mills, Toronto, Ontario.

Published in the United Kingdom by Constable and Company, Ltd., 10 Orange Street, London WC2H 7EG.

This Dover edition, first published in 1983, is a new selection of patterns from *Dorothea Creations,* Vol. 21, published by Alfred Mayer-Weismann & Co., Boston, Mass., in 1941; *Bedspreads to Knit and Crochet,* Book No. 186, published by The Spool Cotton Company, New York, in 1942; *New Table Topics,* Book No. 185, published by The Spool Cotton Company, in 1942; *Crochet Your Gifts,* Book No. 212, published by The Spool Cotton Company, in 1944; *Chair Sets,* Book No. 242, published by The Spool Cotton Company, in 1948; *Pineapple Pageant,* Book No. 252, published by The Spool Cotton Company, in 1948; *Pineapples on Parade,* Book No. 241, published by The Spool Cotton Company, in 1948; *Crochet Charm with Famous DMC Cottons,* Vol. 401, published by The DMC Corporation, in 1950; *Crochet County Fair,* Lily Design Book, No. 51, published by the Lily Mills Co., Shelby, N.C., in 1950; *Royal Society Hand Crochet Doilies,* Book No. 12, published by the Royal Society, Inc., in 1951; *Lily Motifs in Crochet,* Design Book No. 68, published by the Lily Mills Company, in 1953; *Suggestions for Fairs and Bazaars,* Star Book No. 98, published by The American Thread Company, in 1953; *Doilies, Doilies and More Doilies,* Star Doily Book No. 120, published by The American Thread Company, in 1955; *Bedspreads and Tablecloths,* Star Bedspread and Tablecloth Book No. 109, published by The American Thread Company, n.d.; *Crocraft for Cynthia Mercerized Crochet Cottons,* No. 51, published by Cynthia Mills, East Boston, Mass., n.d.; *Doilies,* Star Book No. 44, published by The American Thread Company, n.d.; *Doilies to Treasure,* Lily Book 1600, published by the Lily Mills Company, n.d.; *Things to Crochet for the Home,* Woman's Day Booklet 1951.

Manufactured in the United States of America
Dover Publications, Inc., 180 Varick Street, New York, N.Y. 10014

Library of Congress Cataloging in Publication Data
Main entry under title:

Treasury of pineapple designs for crocheting.

(Dover needlework series)
1. Crocheting—Patterns. I. Macho, Linda, 1955- II. Series. III. Title: Pineapple designs for crocheting.

TT820.T73 1983   746.43'4041   82-18268
ISBN 0-486-24494-6

Introduction

The pineapple has long been the traditional symbol of hospitality and good fortune; perhaps that is why this tropical fruit has been creatively interpreted in such a variety of ways over the years. The pineapple motif was carved into the doors, woodwork and balustrades of many old homes, and has been conventionally used as a carved embellishment on furniture; ornamental ironwork fences and balconies were often garnished with this motif. In colonial times and on into the present day, the actual fruit was a prominent component in wreaths, centerpieces and other home decorations. The pineapple has been featured as a repeating design element on wallpaper and textiles, and needleworkers have made full use of this design in needlepoint as well as in embroidered samplers, doilies and pillowcases. But without a doubt, the most popular and enduring representation of the pineapple is in crochet. Doilies, edgings, vanity sets, placemats, tablecloths, bedspreads, chair sets and even kitchen accessories have all been created with the pineapple as the distinctive design element. Here is a completely new collection of 32 beautiful pineapple crochet patterns originally published over thirty years ago in instruction brochures.

Although many of the threads listed with the patterns are still available, you may wish to substitute some of the newer threads now on the market. Check with your local needlework shop or department and buy thread that is compatible with the recommended hook size. Whatever type of thread you decide to use, be certain to buy a sufficient amount of the same dye lot to complete the project; it is often impossible to match shades later because of the variation in dye lots.

All of the stitches used in the projects in this book are explained on page 5; a list of crochet abbreviations and General Instructions appears on the page facing this one.

For perfect results, the number of stitches and rows should correspond with those indicated in the directions. Before starting any project, make a small sample of the stitch, working with the suggested hook and desired thread. If your working tension is too tight or too loose, use a larger or finer crochet hook to obtain the correct gauge.

When you have completed your project, it should be washed and blocked. No matter how carefully you have worked, blocking will give your pineapple project a "professional" look. Use a good neutral soap or detergent and make suds in warm water. Wash by squeezing the suds through the project, but do not rub. Rinse two or three times in clear water, if desired. Following the measurements given with the pattern, and using rustproof pins, pin the article right side down on a well-padded surface. Be sure to pin out all picots, loops, scallops, etc., along the outside edges. When the project is almost dry, press through a damp cloth with a moderately hot iron. Do not rest the iron on the decorative, raised stitches! When dry, remove pins.

Starching any project will give it a crisper look, and it is essential when finishing the ruffled doilies in this book. Following are excellent directions for starching:

Dissolve ¼ cup starch in ½ cup of cold water. Boil about 1¼ cups of water, remove from flame, then slowly stir the starch mixture into boiling water, stirring constantly. Place back on flame until the mixture thickens. As soon as the starch is cool enough to handle, dip the project and squeeze starch through it thoroughly. Wring out extra starch. The project should be wet with starch but there should be none in the spaces. Pin center of project in position according to size and leave until thoroughly dry. For a ruffled doily, if a steam iron is used, iron ruffle after it is dry; if a regular iron is used, dampen ruffle slightly before pressing. Pin folds of ruffle in position and leave until thoroughly dry.

The crochet terminology and hooks listed in this book are those used in the United States. The charts below give the U.S. name of crochet stitches and their equivalents in other countries and the equivalents to U.S. crochet hook sizes. Crocheters should become familiar with the differences in both crochet terms and hook sizes before starting a project.

Stitch Conversion Chart

U.S. Name	Equivalent
Chain	Chain
Slip	Single crochet
Single crochet	Double crochet
Half-double or short-double crochet	Half-treble crochet
Double crochet	Treble crochet
Treble crochet	Double-treble crochet
Double-treble crochet	Treble-treble crochet
Treble-treble or long-treble crochet	Quadruple-treble crochet
Afghan stitch	Tricot crochet

Hook Conversion Chart

Aluminum

U.S. Size	B	C	D	E	F	G	H	I	J	K
British & Canadian Size	12	11	10	9	8	7	5	4	3	2
Metric Size	2½	3	—	3½	4	4½	5	5½	6	7

Steel

U.S. Size	00	0	1	2	3	4	5	6
British & Canadian Size	000	00	0	1	—	1½	2	2½

METRIC CONVERSION CHART

CONVERTING INCHES TO CENTIMETERS AND YARDS TO METERS

mm — millimeters   cm — centimeters   m — meters

INCHES INTO MILLIMETERS AND CENTIMETERS
(Slightly rounded off for convenience)

inches	mm		cm	inches	cm	inches	cm	inches	cm
⅛	3mm			5	12.5	21	53.5	38	96.5
¼	6mm			5½	14	22	56	39	99
⅜	10mm	or	1cm	6	15	23	58.5	40	101.5
½	13mm	or	1.3cm	7	18	24	61	41	104
⅝	15mm	or	1.5cm	8	20.5	25	63.5	42	106.5
¾	20mm	or	2cm	9	23	26	66	43	109
⅞	22mm	or	2.2cm	10	25.5	27	68.5	44	112
1	25mm	or	2.5cm	11	28	28	71	45	114.5
1¼	32mm	or	3.2cm	12	30.5	29	73.5	46	117
1½	38mm	or	3.8cm	13	33	30	76	47	119.5
1¾	45mm	or	4.5cm	14	35.5	31	79	48	122
2	50mm	or	5cm	15	38	32	81.5	49	124.5
2½	65mm	or	6.5cm	16	40.5	33	84	50	127
3	75mm	or	7.5cm	17	43	34	86.5		
3½	90mm	or	9cm	18	46	35	89		
4	100mm	or	10cm	19	48.5	36	91.5		
4½	115mm	or	11.5cm	20	51	37	94		

YARDS TO METERS
(Slightly rounded off for convenience)

yards	meters	yards	meters	yards	meters	yards	meters	yards	meters
⅛	0.15	2⅛	1.95	4⅛	3.80	6⅛	5.60	8⅛	7.45
¼	0.25	2¼	2.10	4¼	3.90	6¼	5.75	8¼	7.55
⅜	0.35	2⅜	2.20	4⅜	4.00	6⅜	5.85	8⅜	7.70
½	0.50	2½	2.30	4½	4.15	6½	5.95	8½	7.80
⅝	0.60	2⅝	2.40	4⅝	4.25	6⅝	6.10	8⅝	7.90
¾	0.70	2¾	2.55	4¾	4.35	6¾	6.20	8¾	8.00
⅞	0.80	2⅞	2.65	4⅞	4.50	6⅞	6.30	8⅞	8.15
1	0.95	3	2.75	5	4.60	7	6.40	9	8.25
1⅛	1.05	3⅛	2.90	5⅛	4.70	7⅛	6.55	9⅛	8.35
1¼	1.15	3¼	3.00	5¼	4.80	7¼	6.65	9¼	8.50
1⅜	1.30	3⅜	3.10	5⅜	4.95	7⅜	6.75	9⅜	8.60
1½	1.40	3½	3.20	5½	5.05	7½	6.90	9½	8.70
1⅝	1.50	3⅝	3.35	5⅝	5.15	7⅝	7.00	9⅝	8.80
1¾	1.60	3¾	3.45	5¾	5.30	7¾	7.10	9¾	8.95
1⅞	1.75	3⅞	3.55	5⅞	5.40	7⅞	7.20	9⅞	9.05
2	1.85	4	3.70	6	5.50	8	7.35	10	9.15

AVAILABLE FABRIC WIDTHS

25″	65cm	50″	127cm
27″	70cm	54″/56″	140cm
35″/36″	90cm	58″/60″	150cm
39″	100cm	68″/70″	175cm
44″/45″	115cm	72″	180cm
48″	122cm		

AVAILABLE ZIPPER LENGTHS

4″	10cm	10″	25cm	22″	55cm
5″	12cm	12″	30cm	24″	60cm
6″	15cm	14″	35cm	26″	65cm
7″	18cm	16″	40cm	28″	70cm
8″	20cm	18″	45cm	30″	75cm
9″	22cm	20″	50cm		

Simple Crochet Stitches

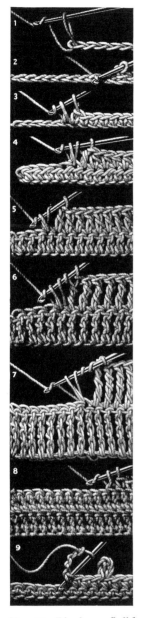

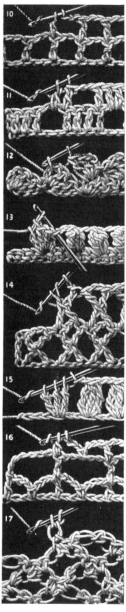

No. 1—Chain Stitch (CH) Form a loop on thread insert hook on loop and pull thread through tightening threads. Thread over hook and pull through last chain made. Continue chains for length desired.

No. 2—Slip Stitch (SL ST) Make a chain the desired length. Skip one chain, * insert hook in next chain, thread over hook and pull through stitch and loop on hook. Repeat from *. This stitch is used in joining and whenever an invisible stitch is required.

No. 3—Single Crochet (S C) Chain for desired length, skip 1 ch, * insert hook in next ch, thread over hook and pull through ch. There are now 2 loops on hook, thread over hook and pull through both loops, repeat from *. For succeeding rows of s c, ch 1, turn insert hook in top of next st taking up both threads and continue same as first row.

No. 4—Short Double Crochet (S D C) Ch for desired length thread over hook, insert hook in 3rd st from hook, draw thread through (3 loops on hook), thread over and draw through all three loops on hook. For succeeding rows, ch 2, turn.

No. 5—Double Crochet (D C) Ch for desired length, thread over hook, insert hook in 4th st from hook, draw thread through (3 loops on hook) thread over hook and pull through 2 loops thread over hook and pull through 2 loops. Succeeding rows, ch 3, turn and work next d c in 2nd d c of previous row. The ch 3 counts as 1 d c.

No. 6—Treble Crochet (TR C) Ch for desired length, thread over hook twice insert hook in 5th ch from hook draw thread through (4 loops on hook) thread over hook pull through 2 loops thread over, pull through 2 loops, thread over, pull through 2 loops. For succeeding rows ch 4, turn and work next tr c in 2nd tr c of previous row. The ch 4 counts as 1 tr c.

No. 7—Double Treble Crochet (D TR C) Ch for desired length thread over hook 3 times insert in 6th ch from hook (5 loops on hook) and work off 2 loops at a time same as tr c. For succeeding rows ch 5 turn and work next d tr c in 2nd d tr c of previous row. The ch 5 counts as 1 d tr c.

No. 8—Rib Stitch. Work this same as single crochet but insert hook in back loop of stitch only. This is sometimes called the slipper stitch.

No. 9—Picot (P) There are two methods of working the picot. (A) Work a single crochet in the foundation, ch 3 or 4 sts depending on the length of picot desired, sl st in top of s c made. (B) Work an s c, ch 3 or 4 for picot and s c in same space. Work as many single crochets between picots as desired.

No. 10—Open or Filet Mesh (O M.) When worked on a chain work the first d c in 8th ch from hook * ch 2, skip 2 sts, 1 d c in next st, repeat from *. Succeeding rows ch 5 to turn, d c in d c, ch 2, d c in next d c, repeat from *.

No. 11—Block or Solid Mesh (S M) Four double crochets form 1 solid mesh and 3 d c are required for each additional solid mesh. Open mesh and solid mesh are used in Filet Crochet.

No. 12—Slanting Shell St. Ch for desired length, work 2 d c in 4th st from hook, skip 3 sts, sl st in next st, * ch 3, 2 d c in same st with sl st, skip 3 sts, sl st in next st. Repeat from *. **2nd Row.** Ch 3, turn 2 d c in sl st, sl st in 3 ch loop of shell in previous row, * ch 3, 2 d c in same space, sl st in next shell, repeat from *.

No. 13—Bean or Pop Corn Stitch. Work 3 d c in same space, drop loop from hook insert hook in first d c made and draw loop through, ch 1 to tighten st.

No. 14—Cross Treble Crochet. Ch for desired length, thread over twice, insert in 5th st from hook, * work off two loops, thread over, skip 2 sts, insert in next st and work off all loops on needle 2 at a time, ch 2, d c in center to complete cross. Thread over twice, insert in next st and repeat from *.

No. 15—Cluster Stitch. Work 3 or 4 tr c in same st always retaining the last loop of each tr c on needle, thread over and pull through all loops on needle.

No. 16—Lacet St. Ch for desired length, work 1 s c in 10th st from hook, ch 3 skip 2 sts, 1 d c in next st, * ch 3, skip 2 sts, 1 s c in next st, ch 3, skip 2 sts 1 d c in next st, repeat from * to end of row, 2nd row, d c in d c, ch 5 d c in next d c.

No. 17—Knot Stitch (Sometimes Called Lovers Knot St.) Ch for desired length, * draw a ¼ inch loop on hook, thread over and pull through ch, s c in single loop of st, draw another ¼ inch loop, s c into loop, skip 4 sts, s c in next st, repeat from *. To turn make ⅜" knots, * s c in loop at right of s c and s c in loop at left of s c of previous row, 2 knot sts and repeat from *.

Pineapple Ruffled Doily

Shown in color on the front cover.

MATERIALS: J. & P. Coats "Knit-Cro-Sheen."
3 balls shaded yellows.
Steel crochet hook No. 2.
Approximate Size: 19 inches in diameter without ruffle.

Ch 6, join to form a ring, ch 1 and work 8 s c in ring, join in 1st s c.
2nd Round. ° Ch 10, s c in next s c, repeat from ° 6 times, ch 4, d tr c (3 times over hook) in next s c (this brings thread in position for next round).
3rd Round. Ch 3, 2 d c in same space, ° ch 7, 3 d c in next loop, repeat from ° all around, ch 7, join.
4th Round. Sl st to next d c, ° ch 5, 3 d c in next loop, ch 5, s c in center d c of next d c group, repeat from ° all around ending with ch 5, 3 d c in next loop, ch 2, tr c in same space with sl st.

5th Round. ° Ch 7, s c in next loop, repeat from ° all around ending with ch 3, tr c in tr c.
6th Round. Ch 6, d c in same space, ° ch 5, 1 d c, ch 3, 1 d c in center st of next loop, repeat from ° all around, ch 5, join in 3rd st of ch.
7th Round. Sl st into loop, ch 3, d c in same space, ch 3, 2 d c in same space, ° ch 3, skip 1 loop, 8 tr c in next loop, ch 3, skip 1 loop, 2 d c, ch 3, 2 d c (shell) in next loop, repeat from ° all around ending with ch 3, skip 1 loop, 8 tr c in next loop, ch 3, join in 3rd st of ch.
8th Round. Sl st into center of shell, ch 3, d c in same space, ch 3, 2 d c in same space, ° ch 3, 1 tr c in each tr c with ch 1 between each tr c, ch 3, 2 d c, ch 3, 2 d c (shell) in center of next shell, repeat from ° all around ending with ch 3, 1 tr c in each tr c with ch 1 between each tr c, ch 3, join in 3rd st of ch.
9th Round. Sl st to center of shell, ch 3, 1 d c, ch 3, 2 d c in

same space, °° ch 4, s c between 1st 2 tr c of pineapple, ° ch 4, s c between next 2 tr c, repeat from ° 5 times, ch 4, 2 d c, ch 3, 2 d c in center of next shell, repeat from °° all around in same manner, join.

10th Round. Sl st to center of shell, ch 3, 1 d c, ch 3, 2 d c in same space, °° ch 4, skip 1 loop, s c in 1st loop of pineapple, ° ch 4, s c in next loop, repeat from ° 4 times, ch 4, shell in next shell, repeat from °° all around in same manner, join.

11th Round. Sl st to center of shell, ch 3, 1 d c, ch 3, 2 d c, ch 3, 2 d c in same space, °° ch 4, s c in 1st loop of pineapple, ° ch 4, s c in next loop, repeat from ° 3 times, ch 4, 2 d c, ch 3, 2 d c, ch 3, 2 d c in center of next shell, repeat from °° all around in same manner, join.

12th Round. Sl st into loop, ch 3, 1 d c, ch 3, 2 d c in same space, °° ch 5, shell in next loop, ch 4, s c in 1st loop of pineapple, ° ch 4, s c in next loop, repeat from ° twice, ch 4, skip 1 loop, shell in next ch 3 loop, repeat from °° all around in same manner, join.

13th Round. Sl st to center of shell, shell in same space, °° ch 3, shell in next loop, ch 3, shell in next shell, ch 4, s c in 1st loop of pineapple, ° ch 4, s c in next loop, repeat from ° once, ch 4, shell in next shell, repeat from °° all around in same manner, join.

14th Round. Sl st to center of shell, shell in same space, ° ch 3, 1 d c, ch 3, 1 d c in next loop, ch 3, shell in next shell, ch 3, 1 d c, ch 3, 1 d c in next loop, ch 3, shell in next shell, ch 4, s c in 1st loop of pineapple, ch 4, s c in next loop, ch 4, shell in next shell, repeat from ° all around in same manner, join.

15th Round. Sl st to center of shell, shell in same space, ° ch 4, skip 1 loop, 8 tr c in next loop, ch 4, shell in next shell, ch 4, skip 1 loop, 8 tr c in next loop, ch 4, shell in next shell, ch 4, s c in remaining loop of pineapple, ch 4, shell in next shell, repeat from ° all around in same manner, join.

16th Round. Sl st to center of shell, shell in same space, ° ch 4, 1 tr c in each of the next 8 tr c with ch 1 between each tr c, ch 4, shell in next shell, ch 4, 1 tr c in each of the next 8 tr c with ch 1 between each tr c, ch 4, shell in next shell, shell in next shell, repeat from ° all around in same manner ending to correspond, join in 3rd st of ch of 1st shell, ch 1, turn.

17th Round. Sl st back to center of shell just made, ch 3, turn, d c in same space, ch 2, 2 d c in center of next shell, °° ch 4, s c between 1st 2 tr c, ° ch 4, s c between next 2 tr c, repeat from ° 5 times, ch 4, shell in next shell, ch 4, s c between 1st 2 tr c, ° ch 4, s c between next 2 tr c, repeat from ° 5 times, ch 4, 2 d c in center of next shell, ch 2, 2 d c in center of next shell, repeat from °° all around in same manner, join.

18th Round. Sl st into ch 2 loop, shell in same space, °° ch 4, s c in 1st loop of pineapple, ° ch 4, s c in next loop, repeat from ° 4 times, ch 4, shell in next shell, ch 4, s c in 1st loop of next pineapple, ° ch 4, s c in next loop, repeat from ° 4 times, ch 4, shell in next ch 2 loop, repeat from °° all around in same manner, join.

19th Round. Sl st to center of shell, ch 3, 1 d c, ch 3, 2 d c, ch 3, 2 d c in same space, °° ch 4, s c in 1st loop of pineapple, ° ch 4, s c in next loop, repeat from ° 3 times, ch 4, 2 d c, ch 3, 2 d c, ch 3, 2 d c in center of next shell, repeat from °° all around in same manner, join.

20th Round. Sl st to loop, shell in same space, °° ch 5, shell in next ch 3 loop, ch 4, s c in 1st loop of pineapple, ° ch 4, s c in next loop, repeat from ° twice, ch 4, shell in next ch 3 loop, repeat from °° all around in same manner, join.

21st Round. Sl st to center of shell, shell in same space, °° ch 4, s c in next loop, ch 4, shell in center of next shell, ch 4, s c in 1st loop of pineapple, ° ch 4, s c in next loop, repeat from ° once, ch 4, shell in next shell, repeat from °° all around in same manner, join.

22nd Round. Sl st to center of shell, shell in same space, ° ch 5, s c in next s c, ch 5, shell in next shell, ch 4, s c in 1st loop of pineapple, ch 4, s c in next loop, ch 4, shell in next shell, repeat from ° all around in same manner, join.

23rd Round. Sl st to center of shell, shell in same space, °° ch 7, ° thread over hook twice, insert in next loop, thread over and work off 2 loops twice, repeat from ° once, thread over and work off all loops at one time, ch 7, shell in next shell, ch 4, s c in remaining loop of pineapple, ch 4, shell in next shell, repeat from °° all around in same manner, join.

24th Round. Sl st to center of shell, shell in same space, ° ch 7, s c in next loop, ch 9, s c in next loop, ch 7, shell in next shell, ch 4, s c in next s c at top of pineapple, ch 4, shell in next shell, repeat from ° all around in same manner, join.

25th Round. Sl st to center of shell, shell in same space, ° ch 7, s c in next loop, ch 7, s c in next loop, ch 7, s c in next loop, ch 7, shell in next shell, ch 1, shell in next shell, repeat from ° all around in same manner, join.

26th Round. Sl st to center of shell, ch 3, d c in same space, °° ch 7, s c in next loop, ° ch 7, s c in next loop, repeat from ° twice, ch 7, 2 d c in center of next shell, 2 d c in center of next shell, repeat from °° all around ending with 2 d c in last shell, join.

27th Round. °° Ch 7, s c in next loop, ° ch 7, s c in next loop, repeat from ° 3 times, ch 7, s c in center of 4 d c group, repeat from °° all around ending with ch 3, tr c in center of 4 d c group.

RUFFLE: ° Ch 10, s c in same loop, ch 10, s c in same loop, ch 10, s c in same loop, ch 10, s c in next loop; repeat from ° all around, ending row with ch 5, tr c in same space as beginning (291 loops).

2nd Round. ° Ch 10, s c in next loop, repeat from ° all around, ending round same as last round. Repeat 2nd round 4 times.

7th Round: Ch 5, sl st in 4th ch from hook for picot, ch 5, ° 4 tr c in next loop, ch 5, sl st in 4th ch from hook for picot, ch 5, s c in next loop. Repeat from ° all around, ending with sl st in base of first picot. Break off.

Palm Tree Delight

ROYAL SOCIETY SIX CORD CORDICHET, Large Ball, *Size 30, 1 ball of White or Ecru.*

Steel Crochet Hook No. 10.

Doily measures 9¼ inches in diameter.

Starting at center, ch 12. Join with sl st to form ring. **1st rnd:** Ch 3, 31 dc in ring. Join. **2nd rnd:** Sc in same place as sl st, * ch 8, skip 3 dc, sc in next dc. Repeat from * around, ending with ch 4, tr in first sc. **3rd rnd:** Ch 4, holding back on hook the last loop of each tr make tr under bar of last tr made, tr in next loop, thread over and draw through all loops on hook (joint-tr made), ch 5, sc in tip of joint-tr (picot made), (ch 4, sc in same loop, ch 4, make a joint-tr in same loop and in next loop, picot) 6 times; ch 4, sc in same loop, ch 4, holding back on hook the last loop of each tr make tr in same loop, 2 tr in top of joining tr on 2nd rnd, thread over and draw through all loops on hook, ch 5, turn; sl st in tip of joint-tr. Turn. **4th rnd:** Sl st in picot, ch 6, holding back on hook the last loop of each tr tr, make tr tr in same picot and in next picot, thread over and draw through all loops on hook, picot, (ch 6, sc in same picot as last tr tr, ch 6,

make a joint-tr tr in same picot and in next picot, make a picot) 6 times; ch 6, sc in same picot, ch 6, holding back on hook the last loop of each tr tr make tr tr in same picot, 2 tr tr in first picot, thread over and draw through all loops on hook, ch 5, turn; sl st in tip of joint-tr tr. Turn. **5th rnd:** Sl st in picot, ch 4, 9 tr in same picot, * ch 9, 10 tr in next picot. Repeat from * around. Join to top of ch-4. **6th rnd:** * Ch 5, (tr in next tr, ch 1) 7 times; tr in next tr, ch 5, sl st in next tr; ch 4, skip 4 ch, sc in next ch, ch 4, sl st in next tr. Repeat from * around. Join at base of ch-5. **7th rnd:** Sl st in next 4 ch, sc in sp, * (ch 4, sc in next sp) 8 times; ch 7, sc in next sp formed by ch-5. Repeat from * around. Join.

8th rnd: Sl st in next loop, sc in same loop, * (ch 4, sc in next loop) 7 times; ch 10, skip next sp, sc in next loop. Repeat from * around. Join. **9th rnd:** Sl st in next loop, sc in same loop, * (ch 4, sc in next loop) 6 times; ch 12, skip next sp, sc in next loop. Repeat from * around. Join. **10th rnd:** Sl st in next loop, sc in same loop, * (ch 4, sc in next loop) 5 times; ch 8, skip 5 ch, dc in next 2 ch, ch 8, sc in next loop. Repeat from * around. Join. **11th rnd:** Sl st in next loop, sc in same loop, * (ch 4, sc in next loop) 4 times; ch 8, 3 tr in each of next 2 dc, ch 8, skip next sp, sc in next loop. Repeat from * around. Join. **12th**

rnd: Sl st in next loop, sc in same loop, * (ch 4, sc in next loop) 3 times; ch 8, skip 6 ch, 2 tr in each of next 2 ch, ch 2, skip 2 tr, 2 tr in each of next 2 tr, ch 2, 2 tr in each of next 2 ch, ch 8, sc in next loop. Repeat from * around. Join. **13th rnd:** Sl st in next loop, sc in same loop, * (ch 4, sc in next loop) twice; ch 8, skip 7 ch, 3 tr in next ch, 2 tr in next tr, (ch 2, 5 tr in next sp) twice; ch 2, skip 3 tr, 2 tr in next tr, 3 tr in next ch, ch 8, sc in next loop. Repeat from * around. Join. **14th rnd:** Sl st in next loop, sc in same loop, * ch 4, sc in next loop, ch 8, skip 7 ch, 3 tr in next ch, 2 tr in next tr, (ch 2, 5 tr in next sp) 3 times; ch 2, skip 4 tr, 2 tr in next tr, 3 tr in next ch, ch 8, sc in next loop. Repeat from * around. Join. **15th rnd:** Sl st to center of next loop, ch 5, * skip 7 ch, 3 tr in next ch, 2 tr in next tr, (ch 2, 5 tr in next sp) 4 times; ch 2, skip 4 tr, 2 tr in next tr, 3 tr in next ch, d tr in next loop. Repeat from * around. Join. **16th rnd:** Ch 4, make a joint-tr in same place as sl st and in next sp, picot, ch 4, sc in same place as last tr, * (ch 4, make a joint-tr in same sp and in next sp, picot, ch 4, sc in same sp as last tr) 4 times; ch 4, make a joint-tr in same sp as last tr and in next d tr, picot, ch 4, sc in same place as last tr, ch 4, make a joint-tr in same place as last tr and in next sp, picot, ch 4, sc in same sp. Repeat from * around. Join and break off. Starch lightly and press.

Sundial

13 Inches in Diameter

MATERIALS: J. & P. Coats or Clark's O.N.T. Best Six Cord Mercerized Crochet, *Size 30:* **Small Ball:** J. & P. Coats—*2 balls of White or Ecru, or 3 balls of any color, or* Clark's O.N.T.—*3 balls of White or Ecru, or 5 balls of any color . . . Steel Crochet Hook No. 10.*

Starting at center ch 16. Join with sl st to form ring. **1st rnd:** Ch 3, 31 dc in ring. Join. **2nd rnd:** Ch 3, dc in each dc around. Join. **3rd rnd:** Ch 3, dc in same place as sl st, 2 dc in each dc around. Join. **4th rnd:** Ch 3, dc in each dc around. Join. **5th rnd:** Sc in same place as sl st, * ch 3, skip 1 dc, sc in next dc. Repeat from * around, ending with ch 3, sl st in first sc. **6th rnd:** Sl st in next ch, sc in loop, ch 7, * tr in next loop, ch 3. Repeat from * around. Join last ch 3 to 4th ch of ch-7. **7th rnd:** Sl st in next ch, sc in same sp, * ch 4, sc in next sp. Repeat from * around. Join. **8th rnd:** Sl st in next 2 ch, sc in same loop, ch 6, * dc in next loop, ch 3. Repeat from * around. Join last ch 3 to 3rd ch of ch-6. **9th rnd:** Ch 4, tr in same place as sl st, * ch 3, 2 tr in next dc. Repeat from * around. Join. **10th rnd:** Ch 4, * 2 tr in next tr, ch 3, tr in next tr. Repeat from * around. Join. **11th rnd:** Ch 4, tr in next 2 tr, * ch 4, tr in next 3 tr. Repeat from * around. Join. **12th to 15th rnds incl:** Repeat 11th rnd, having ch-4 between tr-groups on 12th rnd, ch-5 on 13th rnd, ch-6 on 14th and 15th rnds. **16th rnd:** Ch 4, tr in next 2 tr, * ch 5, (3 tr in next tr) 3 times; ch 5, tr in next 3 tr. Repeat from * around. Join (16 pineapples started on this rnd).

17th rnd: Ch 4, tr in next 2 tr, * ch 3, 3 tr in next tr, tr in next 7 tr, 3 tr in next tr, ch 3, tr in next 3 tr. Repeat from * around. Join. **18th rnd:** Ch 4, tr in next 2 tr, * ch 3, holding back on hook the last loop of each tr make 3 tr in next tr, thread over and draw through all loops on hook (cluster made), ch 3, tr in next 11 tr, ch 3, make a 3-tr cluster in next tr, ch 3, tr in next 3 tr. Repeat from * around. Join. **19th rnd:** Ch 4, tr in next 2 tr, * ch 5, skip cluster and ch-3, cluster in next tr, ch 3, tr in next 9 tr, ch 3, cluster in next tr, ch 5, tr in next 3 tr. Repeat from * around. Join. **20th, 21st and 22nd rnds:** Work as for 19th rnd, having 2 tr less between clusters of pineapples on each rnd and ch-7 before and after each 3-tr group on 20th rnd, ch 9 on 21st rnd and ch-11 on 22nd rnd. **23rd rnd:** Ch 4, make a 2-tr cluster over next 2 tr, * ch 13, make a 3-tr cluster in next tr, ch 3, tr in next tr, ch 3, make a 3-tr cluster in next tr, ch 13, make a 3-tr cluster over next 3 tr. Repeat from * around. Join with sl st to tip of first cluster. **24th rnd:** Ch 4, make a 2-tr cluster in same place as sl st, * ch 17, make a 3-tr cluster in tr between clusters, ch 17, skip next cluster, make a 3-tr cluster in tip of next cluster. Repeat from * around. Join. **25th rnd:** In each loop around make (5 sc, ch 4) 5 times and 5 sc. Join and break off. Starch lightly and press.

Ruffled Cascade

21 Inches in Diameter

MATERIALS: J. & P. COATS OR CLARK'S O.N.T. BEST SIX CORD MERCERIZED CROCHET, *Size 30:* **Small Ball:** J. & P. COATS—*6 balls of White or Ecru, or 8 balls of any color, or* CLARK'S O.N.T.—*8 balls of White or Ecru, or 10 balls of any color . . . Steel Crochet Hook No. 10.*

Starting at center, ch 16. Join with sl st to form ring. **1st rnd:** Ch 3, 31 dc in ring. Sl st in top of ch-3. **2nd rnd:** Sc in same place as sl st, * ch 7, skip 3 dc, sc in next dc. Repeat from * around. Join last ch-7 with sl st to first sc. **3rd rnd:** Sl st in next 3 ch, sc in same loop, * ch 5, holding back on hook the last loop of each tr make tr in same loop as last sc and tr in next loop, thread over and draw through all loops on hook (a joint tr made), ch 5, sl st in tip of joint tr (picot made), ch 5, sc in same loop as last tr of the joint tr was made. Repeat from * around. Join last ch-5 with sl st to first sc. **4th rnd:** Sl st to next picot, sc in same picot, * ch 8, make a joint long tr (5 times over hook), having 1 long tr in same picot as last sc, and the other long tr in the next picot; make a ch-5 picot as before, ch 8, sc in same picot as last long tr of joint long tr. Repeat from * around. Join. **5th rnd:** Sl st to next picot, sl st in picot, ch 5, 9 d tr in same picot, * ch 9, 10 d tr in next picot. Repeat from * around. Join. The d tr groups start the pineapples. **6th rnd:** * Ch 5, tr in next d tr, (ch 1, tr in next d tr) 7 times; ch 5, sc in next d tr, ch 4, sc in center st of next ch-9, ch 4, sc in next d tr. Repeat from * around. Join. **7th rnd:** Sl st in next 4 ch, sc in same

sp, * (ch 4, sc in next sp) 8 times; ch 7, sc in first sp of next pineapple. Repeat from * around. Join with sl st to first sc. **8th rnd:** Sl st in next 2 ch, sc in same loop, * (ch 4, sc in next loop) 7 times; ch 8, sc in next ch-4 loop. Repeat from * around. Join. **9th rnd:** Sl st in next 2 ch, sc in same loop, * (ch 4, sc in next loop) 6 times; ch 13, sc in next ch-4 loop. Repeat from * around. Join.

10th rnd: Sl st in next 2 ch, sc in same loop, * (ch 4, sc in next loop) 5 times; ch 7, skip 5 ch, dc in next 2 ch, ch 7, sc in next ch-4 loop. Repeat from * around. Join. **11th rnd:** Sl st in next 2 ch, sc in same loop, * (ch 4, sc in next loop) 4 times; ch 8, (3 tr in next dc) twice; ch 8, sc in next ch-4 loop. Repeat from * around. Join. **12th rnd:** Sl st in next 2 ch, sc in same loop, * (ch 4, sc in next loop) 3 times; ch 7, skip 6 ch, 2 tr in next 2 ch's, ch 2, skip 2 tr, 2 tr in next 2 tr, ch 2, 2 tr in next 2 ch's, ch 7, sc in next ch-4 loop. Repeat from * around. Join. **13th rnd:** Sl st in next 2 ch, sc in same loop, * (ch 4, sc in next loop) twice; ch 7, 2 tr in last st of next ch, 3 tr in next tr, (ch 2, 5 tr in next sp) twice; ch 2, 3 tr in last tr of next tr group, 2 tr in next ch, ch 7, sc in next ch-4 loop. Repeat from * around. Join. **14th rnd:** Sl st in next 2 ch, sc in same loop, * ch 4, sc in next loop, ch 7, 2 tr in last st of next ch, 3 tr in next tr, (ch 2, 5 tr in next sp) 3 times; ch 2, 3 tr in last tr of next tr group, 2 tr in next ch, ch 7, sc in next ch-4 loop. Repeat from * around. Join. **15th rnd:** Sl st in next 2 ch, sc in same loop, ch 6, * 2 tr in last st of next ch, 3 tr in next tr, (ch 2, 5 tr in next sp) 4 times; ch 2, 3 tr in last tr of next tr group, 2 tr in next ch, tr tr in next ch-4 loop. Repeat

from * around. Join with sl st to top of first ch-6. **16th rnd:** Ch 4, 4 tr in same place as sl st, * (ch 4, 5 tr in next sp) 5 times; ch 4, 5 tr in next tr tr. Repeat from * around. Join. **17th rnd:** Sl st to next sp, ch 4, 4 tr in same sp, * ch 4, 5 tr in next sp. Repeat from * around. Join. **18th and 19th rnds:** Repeat 17th rnd, making ch 5 (instead of ch-4) between tr groups. **20th, 21st and 22nd rnds:** Repeat 17th rnd, making ch 7 (instead of ch-4) between tr groups.

OUTER RUFFLE . . . 1st rnd: Sc in same place as sl st, * (ch 7, skip 1 tr, sc in next tr) twice; ch 7, sc in next sp, (ch 7, sc in same sp) twice; ch 7, sc in next tr. Repeat from * around, ending with ch 3, tr in first sc. **2nd and 3rd rnds:** Ch 10, * dc in next loop, ch 7. Repeat from * around, ending with ch 3, tr in 3rd ch of ch-10. **4th and 5th rnds:** Ch 11, * dc in next loop, ch 8. Repeat from * around, ending with ch 4, tr in 3rd ch of ch-11. **6th and 7th rnds:** Ch 12, * dc in next loop, ch 9. Repeat from * around, ending with ch 4, d tr in 3rd ch of ch-12. **8th rnd:** Ch 13, * dc in next loop, ch 10. Repeat from * around, ending with ch 5, d tr in 3rd ch of ch-13. **9th rnd:** Ch 13, * dc in next loop, ch 10. Repeat from * around. Join and break off.

INNER RUFFLE . . . Attach thread to first tr of any tr group of 15th rnd, sc in same place, * (ch 7, skip 1 tr, sc in next tr) twice; ch 7, sc in next sp (to the right of tr group), ch 7, sc in same sp to the left of same tr group, (ch 7, sc in next tr. Repeat from * around, ending with ch 3, tr in first sc. Repeat 2nd to 7th rnds incl of large Ruffle. Join and break off. Starch lightly and press.

Pineapple Whirlwind

12 Inches Square

MATERIALS: J. & P. Coats or Clark's O.N.T. Best Six Cord Mercerized Crochet, Size 30: **Small Ball:** J. & P. Coats—4 balls of *White or Ecru*, or 6 balls of *any color*, or Clark's O.N.T.—6 balls of *White or Ecru*, or 8 balls of *any color* . . . Steel Crochet Hook No. 10.

GAUGE: Each motif measures 3¾ inches square.

FIRST MOTIF . . . Starting at center, ch 10. Join with sl st to form ring. **1st rnd:** Ch 4, holding back on hook the last loop of each tr, make 2 tr in ring, thread over and draw through all 3 loops on hook (cluster made), * ch 4, holding back on hook the last loop of each tr, make 3 tr in ring, thread over and draw through all loops on hook (another cluster made). Repeat from * until 8 clusters in all are made; ch 4, sl st in tip of first cluster made. **2nd rnd:** Sl st in next ch, sc in sp, ch 4, 2 tr in same sp as last sc, * ch 4, 5 tr in next sp, ch 4, 3 tr in next sp. Repeat from * around, ending with ch 4, sl st in 4th st of ch-4 first made. **3rd rnd:** Ch 3, dc in same place as sl st, * in next tr make dc, ch 2 and dc; 2 dc in next tr, ch 4, sc in next 5 tr, ch 4, 2 dc in next tr. Repeat from * around, ending with ch 4, sl st in 3rd st of ch-3 first made. **4th rnd:** Ch 3, dc in next 2 dc, * in next sp make dc, ch 2 and dc; dc in next 3 dc, (ch 4, sc in next sc) 5 times; ch 4, dc in next 3 dc. Repeat from * around, joining as before. **5th rnd:** Ch 3, dc in next 2 dc, * ch 2, skip next dc, in next sp make 4 dc with ch-2 between; ch 2, skip next dc, dc in next 3 dc, (ch 4, skip next sc, sc in next loop) 4 times; ch 4, dc in next 3 dc. Repeat from * around. Join. **6th rnd:** Ch 3, dc in next 2 dc, * (ch 2, dc in next sp) 3 times; ch 2, dc in same sp; (ch 2, dc in next sp) twice; ch 2, dc in next 3 dc, (ch 4, skip next sc, sc in next loop) 3 times; ch 4, dc in next 3 dc. Repeat from * around. Join. **7th rnd:** Ch 3, dc in next 2 dc, * (ch 2, dc in next sp) 3 times; ch 2, 4 dc in next sp; (ch 2, dc in next sp) 3 times; ch 2, dc in next 3 dc, (ch 4, skip next sc, sc in next loop) twice; ch 4, dc in next 3 dc. Repeat from * around. Join. **8th rnd:** Ch 3, dc in next 2 dc, * (ch 2, dc in next sp) 3 times; ch 2, 4 dc in next sp, ch 3, 4 dc in next sp, (ch 2, dc in next sp) 3 times; ch 2, dc in next 3 dc, ch 4, skip next sc, sc in next loop, ch 4, dc in next 3 dc. Repeat from * around. Join. **9th rnd:** Ch 3, dc in next 2 dc, * (ch 2, dc in next sp) 4 times; ch 2, in next sp make (cluster, ch 2) 3 times and cluster; (ch 2, dc in

next sp) 4 times; ch 2, dc in next 3 dc, skip the next ch-4, the sc and the following ch-4, make dc in next 3 dc. Repeat from * around. Join.
10th rnd: Sl st in next 2 dc, in following 2 ch and in next dc, ch 3, * 2 dc in next sp, dc in next 2 dc, dc in next dc, 2 dc in next sp, dc in next dc, ch 2, dc in tip of next cluster, ch 2, skip next sp and cluster, in next sp make (tr, ch 2) 4 times and tr, ch 2, skip next cluster and sp, dc in tip of next cluster, (ch 2, dc in next dc, 2 dc in next sp, dc in next dc) twice; ch 4, skip next sp, holding back on hook the last loop of each dc, make dc in next 6 dc, thread over and draw through all loops on hook, ch 4, skip next sp, dc in next dc. Repeat from * around. Join and break off.

SECOND MOTIF . . . Work first 9 rnds as for First Motif. **10th rnd:** Work as for 10th rnd of First Motif to the 3rd tr inclusive of first corner, now ch 1, sc in corresponding sp on First Motif, ch 1, tr in same corner sp on Second Motif, ch 2, tr in same sp, ch 1, sc in corresponding sp on First Motif, ch 1, skip next cluster and sp on Second Motif, dc in tip of next cluster, (ch 1, sc in corresponding sp on First Motif, ch 1, dc in next dc on Second Motif, 2 dc in next sp, dc in next dc) twice; ch 2, sc in corresponding sp on First Motif, ch 2, holding back on hook the last loop of each dc, make dc in next 6 dc on Second Motif, thread over and draw through all loops on hook. This completes half of joining. Join other half of this side to correspond and complete remainder of rnd as for First Motif (no more joinings).

Make 2 rows of 2 motifs, joining adjacent sides as Second Motif was joined to First Motif (corner tr's are not joined).

EDGING . . . 1st rnd: Attach thread to center tr at one corner, ch 8 (to count as dc and ch 5), dc in same place as thread was attached, * (ch 2, dc in next tr) twice; (ch 2, dc in next dc) twice (4 sps made over 4 sps); ch 2, skip 2 dc, dc in next dc (sp made over bl), sp over sp, sp over bl, ch 2, dc in next sp, ch 2, dc in tip of cluster, ch 2, dc in next sp, ch 2, dc in next dc, (sp over bl, sp over sp) twice; sp over next 3 sps, ch 2, dc in center tr at corner of next motif. Repeat from * around, making dc, ch 5 and dc at each corner. Join with sl st to 3rd st of ch-8 first made. **2nd to 5th rnds incl:** Sl st to center st of first sp, ch 8, dc in same place as last sl st and work ch-2 sps around, making dc, ch 5 and dc in center st of each corner sp. Join.

OUTER RUFFLE . . . 1st rnd: Sc closely around. Join. **2nd rnd:** Sc in same place as sl st, * ch 5, skip 1 sc, sc in next sc. Repeat from * around. Join. **3rd to 10th rnds incl:** Sl st to center of next loop, sc in same loop, * ch 5, sc in next loop. Repeat from * around. Join. **11th rnd:** Sl st to center of next loop, * ch 7, sc in 4th ch from hook (picot made), ch 3, sc in next loop. Repeat from * around. Join and break off.

INNER RUFFLE . . . Attach thread to corner sp of 1st rnd of Edging and make sc closely along this rnd. Join. Complete Ruffle as for Outer Ruffle. Starch lightly and press.

Pineapples in the Cornfield

14½ Inches in Diameter

MATERIALS: J. & P. Coats or Clark's O.N.T. Best Six Cord Mercerized Crochet, *Size 30, 2 balls (Small Balls) of White, Ecru or any color* . . . Steel Crochet Hook No. 10.

Starting at center, ch 10. Join with sl st to form ring. **1st rnd:** Ch 3, 19 dc in ring. Join with sl st to top of starting chain. **2nd rnd:** Ch 7, skip 1 dc, tr in next dc, * ch 3, skip 1 dc, tr in next dc. Repeat from * around, ending with ch 3, sl st in 4th ch of starting chain. **3rd rnd:** Sl st in next sp, ch 4, holding back on hook the last loop of each tr make 6 tr in same sp, thread over hook and draw through all loops on hook (cluster made); * ch 7, make a 7-tr cluster in next sp. Repeat from * around, ending with ch 4, tr in tip of first cluster. **4th rnd:** * Ch 10, sc in next loop. Repeat from * around, ending with ch 5, d tr in tr. **5th rnd:** Ch 11, tr in next loop, ch 3, tr in same loop, * ch 7, in next loop make tr, ch 3 and tr. Repeat from * around, ending with ch 1, half dc in 7th ch of starting chain. **6th rnd:** Sc in sp formed by ch-1 and the half dc, * ch 7, in next loop make tr, ch 5 and tr; ch 7, sc in next ch-3 sp. Repeat from * around, ending with ch 7, sl st in first sc. **7th rnd:** Sl st in next 7 ch, sl st in next sp, ch 4, make a 4-tr cluster in same sp, * (ch 5, make 5-tr cluster in same sp) twice; ch 9, 5-tr cluster in next ch-3 sp. Repeat from * around, ending with ch 9, sl st in tip of first cluster. **8th rnd:** Sl st to center of first ch-5 loop, sc in same loop, * ch 7, sc in next ch-5 loop, ch 7, sc in next ch-9 loop, ch 7, sc in next ch-5 loop. Repeat from * around, ending with ch 3, tr in first sc.

9th rnd: * Ch 7, sc in next loop. Repeat from * around, ending with ch 3, tr in tr. **10th rnd:** * Ch 9, sc in next loop. Repeat from * around, ending with ch 4, d tr in tr. **11th rnd:** Repeat 10th rnd, ending with ch 4, d tr in d tr. **12th rnd:** * Ch 12, sc in next loop. Repeat from * around, ending with ch 12, sl st in d tr. **13th rnd:** Sl st in next 6 ch, ch 4, 2 tr in same place as last sl st, * ch 3, 3 tr in next ch, ch 5, 4 tr in 6th ch and 5 tr in 7th ch of next loop, ch 5, 3 tr in 6th ch of next loop. Repeat from * around, ending with ch 5, sl st in top of starting chain. **14th rnd:** Sl st in next 2 tr, sl st in next ch-3 sp, ch 4, 2 tr in same sp, * ch 3, 3 tr in same sp (shell made over shell), ch 5, (tr in next tr, ch 1) 8 times; tr in next tr, ch 5, 3 tr in next ch-3 sp. Repeat from * around. Join. **15th rnd:** Sl st to next ch-3 sp, ch 4 and complete shell as before,

* ch 5, sc in next ch-1 sp, (ch 5, sc in next sp) 7 times; ch 5, in next ch-3 sp make 3 tr, ch 3 and 3 tr (shell over shell). Repeat from * around. Join. **16th rnd:** Sl st to first ch-3 sp, ch 4 and complete shell as before, * ch 5, skip next ch-5, sc in next ch-5 loop, (ch 5, sc in next ch-5 loop) 6 times; ch 5, shell over shell. Repeat from * around. Join. **17th rnd:** * Make shell over shell as before, ch 5, skip next ch-5, sc in next ch-5 loop, (ch 5, sc in next ch-5 loop) 5 times; ch 5. Repeat from * around. Join. **18th rnd:** * Shell over shell, ch 5, skip next ch-5, sc in next ch-5 loop, (ch 5, sc in next loop) 4 times; ch 5. Repeat from * around. Join.

19th rnd: Sl st to next ch-3 sp, ch 4, in same sp make 2 tr, (ch 3, 3 tr) twice; * ch 5, skip next ch-5, sc in next ch-5 loop, (ch 5, sc in next loop) 3 times; ch 5, in sp of next shell make (3 tr, ch 3) twice and 3 tr. Repeat from * around. Join. **20th rnd:** Sl st to next ch-3 sp, ch 4 and complete shell in same sp, * shell in next sp, ch 5, skip next ch-5, sc in next ch-5 loop, (ch 5, sc in next loop) twice; ch 5, shell in next ch-3 sp. Repeat from * around. Join. **21st rnd:** * Shell over shell, ch 7, shell over shell, ch 5, skip next ch-5, sc in next ch-5 loop, ch 5, sc in next loop, ch 5. Repeat from * around. Join. **22nd rnd:** * Shell over shell, ch 5, in 4th ch of next ch-7 make tr, ch 5 and tr; ch 5, shell over shell, ch 5, skip next ch-5, sc in next ch-5 loop, ch 5. Repeat from * around. Join. **23rd rnd:** * Shell over shell, ch 5, skip next sp, (in next sp make a 5-d tr cluster, ch 5) twice and 5 d tr cluster; ch 5, shell over shell, ch 5, sc in next sc, ch 5. Repeat from * around. Join. **24th rnd:** * Shell over shell, (ch 7, sc in next loop), 4 times; ch 5, shell over shell, ch 3. Repeat from * around. Join. **25th rnd:** Sl st to next sp, sc in same ch-3 sp, * (ch 8, sc in next loop) 5 times; ch 8, sc in next ch-3 sp, 3 tr in next sp (between shells), ch 4, sl st in 4th ch from hook (picot made), 3 tr in same sp, sc in sp of next shell. Repeat from * around. Join and break off. Starch lightly and press.

Hawaiian Sunburst

11½ Inches in Diameter

MATERIALS: J. & P. Coats or Clark's O.N.T. Best Six Cord Mercerized Crochet, *Size 30, 2 balls (Small Balls) of White, Ecru or any color . . . Steel Crochet Hook No. 10.*

Starting at center, ch 10. Join with sl st to form ring. **1st rnd:** Ch 3, 23 dc in ring. Sl st in top of ch-3. **2nd rnd:** Sc in same place as sl st, * ch 5, skip 1 dc, sc in next dc. Repeat from * around, ending with ch 5, sl st in first sc. **3rd rnd:** Sl st in next 2 ch, sc in same loop, * ch 5, holding back on hook the last loop of each tr make 3 tr in next loop, thread over and draw through all loops on hook (cluster made), (ch 3, cluster in same loop) twice; ch 5, sc in next loop. Repeat from * around, joining last ch-5 with sl st in first sc. **4th rnd:** Sl st to center

of next loop, sc in same loop, * ch 5, in next loop make cluster, ch 3 and cluster; ch 3, in next loop make cluster, ch 3 and cluster; (ch 5, sc in next loop) twice. Repeat from * around. Join. **5th rnd:** Sl st to center of next loop, sc in same loop, * ch 5, sc in next loop. Repeat from * around. Join. **6th and 7th rnds:** Repeat 5th rnd. **8th rnd:** Sl st in next loop, ch 3, 4 dc in same loop, 5 dc in each loop around. Join (180 dc, counting starting chain as 1 dc). **9th rnd:** Sl st in next 7 dc, ch 3, in same place as last sl st make dc, ch 2 and 2 dc (shell made); * in center dc of next 5-dc group make 2 dc, ch 2 and 2 dc (another shell made). Repeat from * around. Join.

10th rnd: Sl st in next dc and in next sp, ch 3, in same sp make dc, ch 2 and 2 dc (shell made over shell), * ch 1, in sp of next shell make 2 dc, ch 2 and 2 dc (another shell made over shell). Repeat from * around, ending with ch 1, sl st in top of ch-3. **11th rnd:** * Shell over shell. Repeat from * around. Join. **12th rnd:** * Shell over shell, ch 3, sc in sp of next shell, ch 2, shell in next sp, ch 2, sc in sp of next shell, ch 3. Repeat from * around. Join. **13th rnd:** * Shell over shell, ch 3, in sp of next shell make 2 dc, ch 5 and 2 dc; ch 3. Repeat from * around. Join. **14th rnd:** * Shell over shell, ch 2, 12 tr in next ch-5 sp, ch 2. Repeat from * around. Join. **15th rnd:**

* Shell over shell, ch 2, (tr in next tr, ch 1) 11 times; tr in next tr, ch 2. Repeat from * around. Join. **16th rnd:** * Shell over shell, ch 3, sc in next ch-1 sp, (ch 3, sc in next sp) 10 times; ch 3. Repeat from * around. Join. **17th rnd:** * Shell over shell, ch 4, skip next ch-3, sc in next ch-3 loop, (ch 3, sc in next loop) 9 times; ch 4. Repeat from * around. Join. **18th rnd:** * Shell over shell, ch 4, sc in next ch-3 loop, (ch 3, sc in next ch-3 loop) 8 times; ch 4. Repeat from * around. Join. **19th rnd:** * Shell over shell, ch 4, sc in next ch-3 loop, (ch 3, sc in next loop) 7 times; ch 4. Repeat from * around. Join.

20th rnd: Sl st in next dc and in sp, ch 3, in same sp make dc and (ch 2, 2 dc) twice; * ch 4, sc in next ch-3 loop, (ch 3, sc in next loop) 6 times; ch 4, 2 dc in sp of next shell, in same sp make (ch 2, 2 dc) twice. Repeat from * around. Join. **21st rnd:** Sl st in next dc and in next sp, ch 3, in same sp make dc, ch 2 and 2 dc (shell made); * shell in next sp, ch 4, sc in next ch-3 loop, (ch 3, sc in next loop) 5 times; ch 4, shell in next ch-2 sp. Repeat from * around. Join. **22nd rnd:** * Shell over shell, ch 2, shell over shell, ch 4, sc in next ch-3 loop, (ch 3, sc in next loop) 4 times; ch 4. Repeat from * around. Join. **23rd rnd:** * Shell over shell, shell in next ch-2 sp, shell over shell, ch 4, sc in next ch-3 loop, (ch 3, sc in next loop) 3 times; ch 4. Repeat from * around. Join. **24th rnd:** Sl st in next dc and in sp, ch 3, dc in same sp, (ch 2, 2 dc in same sp) twice; * ch 2, shell over shell, ch 2, in sp of next shell make 2 dc, (ch 2, 2 dc) twice; ch 4, sc in next ch-3 loop, (ch 3, sc in next loop) twice; ch 4, in next ch-2 sp make 2 dc, (ch 2, 2 dc) twice. Repeat from * around. Join.

25th rnd: Sl st in next dc and in next sp, ch 3, in same sp make dc, ch 2 and 2 dc; * shell in next sp, ch 2, shell over shell, ch 2, skip next sp, (shell in next sp) twice; ch 4, sc in next ch-3 loop, ch 3, sc in next loop, ch 4, shell in next ch-2 sp. Repeat from * around. Join. **26th rnd:** * Shell over shell, (ch 2, shell over shell) 4 times; ch 4, sc in next ch-3 loop, ch 4. Repeat from * around. Join. **27th rnd:** * (Shell over shell, ch 2) twice; in sp of next shell make 2 dc, (ch 2, 2 dc) twice; (ch 2, shell over shell) twice. Repeat from * around. Join. **28th rnd:** Sl st in next dc, and in next sp, sc in same sp, * ch 7, dc in sp of next shell, ch 7, skip next ch-2, in next sp make a 3-tr cluster, ch 3, cluster in next sp, ch 7, dc in sp of next shell, ch 7, sc in sp of next shell, ch 2, sc in sp of next shell. Repeat from * around. Join. **29th rnd:** Sl st in next 3 ch, sc in same sp, * ch 7, dc in next sp, ch 7, in sp between clusters make (cluster, ch 2) twice and cluster; ch 7, dc in next sp, ch 7, sc in next sp, ch 5, sc in next ch-2 sp, ch 5, sc in next sp. Repeat from * around. Join. **30th rnd:** Sl st in next 3 ch, sc in same sp, * ch 7, dc in next sp, ch 7, (cluster in next ch-2 sp) twice; ch 7, dc in next sp, ch 7, sc in next sp, ch 5, sc in next sp, ch 3, sc in next sp, ch 5, sc in next sp. Repeat from * around. Join and break off. Starch lightly and press. ☙

Golden Pineapples

Shown in color on the inside front cover.

Materials Required: AMERICAN THREAD COMPANY
The Famous "PURITAN" MERCERIZED CROCHET COTTON, Article 40
3 balls Shaded Yellows
2 balls White or colors of your choice
Steel crochet hook No. 7
Approximate size: 26 inches in diameter or

"GEM" MERCERIZED CROCHET COTTON, Article 35, size 30
2 balls Shaded Yellows
1 ball White or colors of your choice
Steel crochet hook No. 12
Approximate size: 19 inches in diameter

With White ch 6, join to form a ring, ch 1 and work 8 s c in ring, join in 1st s c.

2nd Round. Ch 3, d c in same space, ° ch 2, 2 d c in next s c, repeat from ° all around, ch 2, join in 3rd st of ch.

3rd Round. ° Ch 10, s c in next d c, 1 s c, ch 3, 1 s c in next ch 2 loop, s c in next d c, repeat from ° all around ending with ch 10, s c in next d c, 1 s c, ch 3, 1 s c in next ch 2 loop.

4th Round. Sl st to center of next loop, ch 3, 4 d c in same space, ° ch 7, 5 d c in next ch 10 loop, repeat from ° all around, ch 7, join.

5th Round. Sl st to center d c of 1st d c group, ° ch 3, s c in same space, ch 3, d c in center st of next loop, ch 5, d c in same space, ch 3, s c in center d c of next d c group, repeat from ° 6 times, ch 3, s c in same space, ch 3, d c in center st

of next loop, ch 5, d c in same space, ch 3, join in same space as beginning.

6th Round. Sl st to ch 5 loop, ch 3, 2 d c in same space keeping last loop of each d c on hook, thread over and work off all loops at one time, ° ch 4, cluster st in same space (cluster st: 3 d c in same space keeping last loop of each d c on hook, thread over and work off all loops at one time), repeat from ° twice, ° ch 7, 4 cluster sts with ch 4 between each cluster st in next ch 5 loop, repeat from ° all around, ch 7, join.

7th Round. Sl st into 1st ch 4 loop, ° ch 5, s c in next loop, ch 5, s c in next loop, ch 5, s c in center st of next loop, ch 5, s c in next loop, repeat from ° all around ending with ch 2, d c in sl st.

8th Round. ° Ch 5, s c in next loop, repeat from ° all around ending with ch 2, d c in d c.

9th Round. Ch 8, d c in same space, ° ch 3, s c in center st of next loop, ch 3, s c in same space, ch 3, 1 d c, ch 5, 1 d c in center st of next loop, repeat from ° all around ending with ch 3, s c in center st of next loop, ch 3, s c in same space, ch 3, join in 3rd st of ch 8, cut White.

10th Round. Attach Shaded Yellows in any ch 5 loop directly over the 4 cluster group of 6th round, ch 3, 2 d c, ch 3, 3 d c in same space, ° ch 5, 9 tr c in next ch 5 loop, ch 5, 3 d c, ch 3, 3 d c (shell) in next ch 5 loop, repeat from ° all around ending with ch 5, 9 tr c in next ch 5 loop, ch 5, join.

11th Round. Sl st to center of shell, ch 3 (counts as part of 1st shell), 2 d c, ch 3, 3 d c in same space, ° ch 5, 1 tr c in each of the next 9 tr c with ch 1 between each tr c, ch 5, 3 d c, ch 3, 3 d c (shell) in center of next shell (all shells will be made in same manner for remainder of doily except where stated otherwise), repeat from ° all around ending to correspond, ch 5, join.

12th Round. Sl st to center of shell, ch 3, shell in same space, °° ch 5, s c between 1st 2 tr c, ° ch 4, s c in next ch 1 space. repeat from ° 6 times, ch 5, shell in next shell, repeat from °° all around ending to correspond, ch 5, join.

13th Round. Sl st to center of shell, ch 3, shell in same space, ch 3, 3 d c in same space, °° ch 5, skip 1 loop, s c in next loop, ° ch 4, s c in next loop, repeat from ° 5 times, ch 5, shell in next shell, ch 3, 3 d c in same space, repeat from °° all around ending to correspond, ch 5, join.

14th Round. Sl st across 1st 3 d c, across ch and next 3 d c and into next loop, ch 3, shell in same space, °° ch 5, skip 1 loop, s c in next loop, ° ch 4, s c in next loop, repeat from ° 4 times, ch 5, shell in 1st ch 3 loop of next shell, ch 1, turn, sl st to center of shell, ch 3, shell in same space, ch 5, skip 1 loop, s c in next loop, work 4-ch 4 loops across pineapple, ch 5, shell in next shell, ch 1, turn, sl st to center of shell, ch 3, shell in same space, ch 5, skip 1 loop, s c in next loop, work 3-ch 4 loops across pineapple, ch 5, shell in next shell, ch 1, turn, sl st to center of shell, ch 3, shell in same space, ch 5, skip 1 loop, s c in next loop, work 2-ch 4 loops across pineapple, ch 5, shell in next shell, ch 1, turn, sl st to center of shell, ch 3, shell in same space, ch 5, skip 1 loop, s c in next loop, ch 4, s c in next loop, ch 5, shell in next shell, ch 1, turn, sl st to center of shell, ch 3, shell in same space, ch 5, s c in remaining loop of pineapple, ch 5, shell in next shell, ch 1, turn, sl st to center of shell, ch 3, shell in same space, shell in next shell, ch 1, turn, sl st to center of shell, ch 3, 2 d c in same space, 3 d c in center of next shell, cut thread.

With right side of work toward you, attach Shaded Yellows in next ch 3 loop of same divided shell of 13th round, ch 3, shell in same space, repeat from °° 7 times (8 pineapples completed).

1st Row around Pineapples. With right side of work toward you attach White in 1st d c at top of pineapple, ch 6, d c in same space, °° ch 3, skip 4 d c, 1 d c, ch 3, 1 d c in next st, ° ch 3 and working down side of pineapple, skip 1 row, 1 d c, ch 3, 1 d c in point of next row, repeat from ° twice, skip last row of same pineapple and 1st row on side of next pineapple, 1 d c, ch 3, 1 d c (single shell) in point of next row, ° ch 3, skip 1 row, 1 d c, ch 3, 1 d c in point of next row, repeat from ° twice, repeat from °° all around ending to correspond, ch 3, join in 3rd st of ch.

2nd Round. Sl st into loop, ch 3, 2 d c in same space keeping last loop of each d c on hook, thread over and work off all loops at one time, ch 3, cluster st in same space, °° ch 4, 1 d c, ch 3, 1 d c in center st of next loop, ch 4, 2 cluster sts with ch 3 between in next loop, ° ch 4, skip 1 loop, 1 d c, ch 3, 1 d c in next loop, repeat from ° once, ch 4, skip 1 loop, cluster st in next loop, ch 1, cluster st in next loop, ° ch 4, skip 1 loop, 1 d c, ch 3, 1 d c in next loop, repeat from ° once, ch 4, skip 1 loop, 2 cluster sts with ch 3 between in next loop, repeat from °° all around ending to correspond, ch 4, join in 1st cluster st.

3rd Round. Sl st into loop, ch 3 (counts as part of 1st cluster st at beginning of each round), cluster st in same space, ch 3, cluster st in same space, °° ch 4, skip 1 loop, 5 d c with ch 1 between each d c in next loop, ch 4, skip 1 loop, 2 cluster sts with ch 3 between in next loop, ° ch 4, single shell in next single shell, repeat from ° once, ch 3, cluster st in ch 1 space between next 2 cluster sts, ch 3, sl st in top of cluster st for picot, ch 3, single shell in next single shell, ch 4, single shell in next single shell, ch 4, 2 cluster sts with ch 3 between in loop between next 2 cluster sts, repeat from °° all around ending to correspond, ch 4, join.

4th Round. Sl st to center of shell, ch 3, 2 cluster sts with ch 3 between in same space, °° ch 4, 1 d c in each of the next 5 d c with ch 3 between each d c, ch 4, 2 cluster sts with ch 3 between in loop between next 2 cluster sts, ch 4, single shell in next single shell, ch 4, 2 cluster sts with ch 3 between in next single shell, ch 1, 2 cluster sts with ch 3 between in next single shell, ch 4, single shell in next single shell, ch 4, 2 cluster sts with ch 3 between in loop between

next 2 cluster sts, repeat from °° all around ending to correspond, ch 4, join.

5th Round. Sl st to center of shell, ch 3, 2 cluster sts with ch 3 between in same space, ° ch 4, 1 d c in each of the next 5 d c with ch 4 between each d c, ch 4, 2 cluster sts with ch 3 between in loop between next 2 cluster sts, ch 4, single shell in next single shell, ch 4, cluster st between next 2 cluster sts, ch 1, cluster st between next 2 cluster sts, ch 4, single shell in next single shell, ch 4, 2 cluster sts with ch 3 between in loop between next 2 cluster sts, repeat from ° all around ending to correspond, ch 4, join.

6th Round. Sl st to center of shell, ch 3, 2 cluster sts with ch 3 between in same space, ° ch 4, 1 d c in each of the next 3 d c with ch 4 between each d c, ch 4, d c in same space, ch 4, 1 d c in each of the next 2 d c with ch 4 between each d c, ch 4, skip 1 loop, 2 cluster sts with ch 3 between in next loop, ch 4, single shell in next single shell, ch 4, skip 1 loop, cluster st in ch 1 space between next 2 cluster sts, ch 3, sl st in top of cluster st for picot, ch 4, single shell in next single shell, ch 4, skip 1 loop, 2 cluster sts with ch 3 between in loop between next 2 cluster sts, repeat from ° all around ending to correspond, ch 4, join.

7th Round. Sl st to center of shell, ch 3, 2 cluster sts with ch 3 between in same space, ° ch 4, d c in next d c, ch 4, d c in next d c, ch 4, skip 1 loop, 5 d c with ch 3 between each d c in next loop, ch 4, skip 1 loop, d c in next d c, ch 4, d c in next d c, ch 4, 2 cluster sts with ch 3 between in loop between next 2 cluster sts (cluster st shell), ch 4, cluster st shell in next single shell, ch 4, cluster st shell in next single shell, ch 4, cluster st shell in next cluster st shell, repeat from ° all around ending to correspond, ch 4, join.

8th Round. Sl st to center of shell, ch 3, 2 cluster sts with ch 3 between in same space, ° ch 4, 1 d c in each of the next 9 d c with ch 4 between each d c, ch 4, cluster st shell in next cluster st shell, ch 4, cluster st shell in next cluster st shell, ch 2, cluster st shell in next cluster st shell, ch 4, cluster st shell in next cluster st shell, repeat from ° all around ending to correspond, ch 4, join.

9th Round. Sl st to center of shell, ch 3, 2 cluster sts with ch 3 between in same space, ° ch 5, 1 d c in each of the next 9 d c with ch 5 between each d c, ch 5, cluster st shell in next cluster st shell, ch 4, cluster st in center of next cluster st shell, ch 1, cluster st in center of next cluster st shell, ch 4, cluster st shell in next cluster st shell, repeat from ° all around ending to correspond, ch 4, join.

10th Round. Sl st to center of shell, ch 3, 2 cluster sts with ch 3 between in same space, ° ch 6, 1 d c in each of the next 9 d c with ch 6 between each d c, ch 6, cluster st shell in next cluster st shell, ch 4, skip 1 loop, cluster st in next ch 1 space, ch 3, sl st in top of cluster st for picot, ch 4, cluster st shell in next cluster st shell, repeat from ° all around ending to correspond, ch 4, join.

11th Round. Sl st to center of shell, ch 3, 2 cluster sts with ch 3 between in same space, ° ch 6, 1 d c in each of the next 9 d c with ch 6 between each d c, ch 6, cluster st shell in next cluster st shell, ch 4, cluster st shell in next cluster st shell, repeat from ° all around ending to correspond, ch 4, join.

12th Round. Sl st to center of shell, ch 3, 2 cluster sts with ch 3 between in same space, ° ch 7, 1 d c in each of the next 9 d c with ch 7 between each d c, ch 7, cluster st shell in next cluster st shell, ch 1, cluster st shell in next cluster st shell, repeat from ° all around ending to correspond, ch 1, join.

13th Round. Sl st to center of shell, ch 3, cluster st in same space, °° ch 7, 1 d c, ch 3, 1 d c in next d c, ° ch 5, 1 d c, ch 3, 1 d c in next d c, repeat from ° 7 times, ch 7, cluster st in center of next cluster st shell, ch 1, cluster st in next cluster st shell, repeat from °° all around ending to correspond, ch 1, join.

14th Round. Ch 3, cluster st in the ch 1 space just made, °° ch 3, sl st in top of cluster st for picot, ch 7, single shell in next single shell, ° ch 5, single shell in next single shell, repeat from ° 7 times, ch 7, cluster st between next 2 cluster sts, repeat from °° all around ending to correspond, ch 7, join, cut thread.

15th Round. Attach Shaded Yellows in any picot, ch 3, 2 d c, ch 3, 3 d c in same space, ° ch 5, skip 1 loop, 3 s c in next

(continued on page 48)

Palm Fronds

12½ Inches in Diameter

MATERIALS: J. & P. Coats or Clark's O.N.T. Best Six Cord Mercerized Crochet, *Size 50, 2 balls of White only . . . Steel Crochet Hook No. 12 . . . A piece of linen 4 inches square.*

Cut linen into a circle 4 inches in diameter. **1st rnd:** Turn edges ¼ inch under and make 144 sc in all around. Sl st in first sc. **2nd rnd:** Sc in same place as sl st, * ch 3, skip next sc, sc in next sc. Repeat from * around, ending with ch 3, sl st in first sc (72 loops). **3rd rnd:** Sl st in next 2 ch, ch 3, dc in next loop, ch 7, thread over hook 3 times, insert hook in next loop, thread over and draw loop through, (thread over and draw through 2 loops) twice; thread over hook twice, insert hook in next loop, thread over and draw loop through, (thread over and draw through 2 loops) 5 times—joint tr made; * ch 5, make a joint tr in next 2 loops. Repeat from * around, ending with ch 5, sl st in the 2nd ch of ch-7 (36 sps). **4th rnd:** Sl st in sp, ch 4, in same sp make 2 tr, ch 1 and 3 tr; * ch 6, skip next joint tr, sc in next joint tr, ch 6, skip next joint tr, in next sp make 3 tr, ch 1 and 3 tr. Repeat from * around, ending with ch 6, sl st in 4th ch of ch-4.

5th rnd: Ch 4, tr in next 2 tr, * ch 1, tr in next 3 tr, (ch 5, sc in next loop) twice; ch 5, tr in next 3 tr. Repeat from * around, sl st in 4th ch of ch-4. **6th rnd:** Ch 4, tr in next 2 tr, * ch 1, tr in next 3 tr, ch 8, skip 1 loop, sc in next loop, ch 8, tr in the next 3 tr. Repeat from * around. Join. **7th rnd:** Ch 4, tr in next 2 tr, * ch 3, in next ch-1 sp make tr, ch 3 and tr; ch 3, tr in next 3 tr, ch 9, tr in next 3 tr. Repeat from * around, ending with ch 9. Join. **8th rnd:** Ch 4, tr in the next 2 tr, * ch 3, skip next ch-3, in ch-3 loop between next 2 tr make 12 tr, ch 3, skip next sp, tr in next 3 tr, ch 7, tr in next 3 tr. Repeat from * around, ending with ch 7. Join. **9th rnd:** Ch 4, tr in next 2 tr, * ch 4, (tr in next tr, ch 1) 11 times; tr in next tr, ch 4, tr in next 3 tr, ch 3, tr in next 3 tr. Repeat from * around. Join. **10th rnd:** Ch 4, tr in next 2 tr, * ch 5, sc in ch-1 sp between next 2 tr, (ch 3, sc in next sp) 10 times; ch 5, tr in next 3 tr, skip next ch-3, tr in the next 3 tr. Repeat from * around, ending with tr in last 3 tr. Join. **11th rnd:** Ch 3, dc in the next 2 tr, * ch 5, sc in the next ch-3 loop, (ch 3, sc in next loop) 9 times; ch 5, dc in the next 6 tr. Repeat from * around, ending with dc in last 3 tr, sl st in 3rd ch of ch-3.

12th rnd: Ch 3, dc in next 2 dc, * ch 5, sc in next ch-3 loop, (ch 3, sc in next loop) 8 times; ch 5, dc in next 6 dc. Repeat from * around. Join. **13th rnd:** Ch 3, dc in next 2 dc, * ch 5, sc in next ch-3 loop, (ch 3, sc in next loop) 7 times; ch 5, dc in next 3 dc, ch 2, dc in next 3 dc. Repeat from * around. Join. **14th rnd:** Ch 3, dc in next 2 dc, * ch 5, sc in next ch-3 loop, (ch 3, sc in next loop) 6 times; ch 5, dc in next 3 dc, ch 4, dc in next 3 dc. Repeat from * around. Join. **15th rnd:** Ch 3, dc in next 2 dc, * ch 5, sc in next ch-3 loop, (ch 3, sc in next loop) 5 times; ch 5, dc in next 3 dc, ch 5, dc in next 3 dc. Repeat from * around. Join. **16th rnd:** Ch 3, dc in next 2 dc, * ch 5, sc in next ch-3 loop, (ch 3, sc in next loop) 4 times; ch 5, dc in next 3 dc, ch 4, sc in next loop, ch 4, dc in next 3 dc. Repeat from * around. Join. **17th rnd:** Ch 3, dc in next 2 dc, * ch 5, sc in next ch-3 loop, (ch 3, sc in next loop) 3 times; ch 5, dc in the next 3 dc, ch 3, sc in next loop, ch 5, sc in next loop, ch 3, dc in next 3 dc. Repeat from * around. Join.

18th rnd: Ch 3, dc in next 2 dc, * ch 5, sc in next ch-3 loop, (ch 3, sc in next loop) twice; ch 5, dc in next 3 dc, ch 6, skip 1 loop, sc in next loop, ch 6, skip next loop, dc in next 3 dc. Repeat from * around. Join. **19th rnd:** Ch 4, tr in next 2 dc, * ch 5, sc in next ch-3 loop, ch 3, sc in next ch-3 loop, ch 5, tr in next 3 dc, ch 6, sc in next loop twice; ch 6, tr in next 3 dc. Repeat from * around. Sl st in 4th ch of ch-4. **20th rnd:** Ch 4, tr in next 2 tr, * ch 5, sc in next ch-3 loop, ch 5, tr in next 3 tr, (ch 6, sc in next loop) 3 times; ch 6, tr in next 3 tr. Repeat from * around. Join. **21st rnd:** Ch 4, tr in next 2 tr, * ch 5, tr in next 3 tr, * (ch 6, sc in next loop) 4 times; ch 6, tr in next 6 tr. Repeat from * around. Join. **22nd rnd:** Ch 4, holding back on hook the last loop of each tr make tr in next 5 tr, thread over and draw through all loops on hook (cluster made), * (ch 7, sc in the next loop) 5 times; ch 7, make a cluster over the next 6 tr as before. Repeat from * around, ending with ch 3, tr in tip of cluster. **23rd rnd:** * Ch 8, sc in the next loop. Repeat from * around, ending with ch 4, d tr in tr. **24th rnd:** * Ch 9, sc in next loop. Repeat from * around, ending with ch 9, sl st in d tr. Break off. Starch lightly and press.

Pineapple Lace Edging

Approximate Sizes: Small Round Doily, 12½ inches, Oval Doily, 12 inches by 17½ inches, Large Round Doily, 17 inches.

MATERIALS — D·M·C Crochet Superba, Art. 163; Size 30 or Size 40, White, Ecru or Ivory (Size 30 also in Colors).

Oval Doily, 1½ balls; Small Round Doily, 1 ball; Large Round Doily, 1½ balls.

Suitable linen for centers.

Steel Crochet Hook, Size 12.

GAUGE: 4 chs = ¼ inch

PINEAPPLE LACE EDGING—Row 1 (Wrong side)—Ch 33, 1 sc in 2nd ch from hook, 1 sc in each of next 7 chs, * ch 5, skip 3 chs, 1 sc in next ch; rpt from STAR 4 times, ch 5, skip 3 chs, work a Shell of [3 dc, ch 2, 3 dc] all in last ch. **Row 2**—Ch 5, turn, work a Shell of [3 dc, ch 2, 3 dc] all in ch-2 of first Shell, ch 5, skip next loop, [1 dc, ch 6, 1 dc] all in next loop, ch 5, skip next loop, a Shell in next loop, 1 sc in next loop, ch 5, 1 sc in next loop, ch 5, skip 2 sc, slip st in each of next 6 sc. **Row 3**—Ch 10, turn, 1 sc in first loop, ch 5, 1 sc in next loop, ch 5, a Shell in ch-2 sp of next Shell, ch 4, skip next ch-5, work 14 tr in ch-6 loop for Base of Pineapple, ch 4, skip next ch-5, a Shell in ch-2 sp of next Shell. **Row 4**—Ch 5, turn, a Shell in first Shell, ch 4, 1 sc in each of next 14 tr, ch 4, a Shell in next Shell, [ch 5, 1 sc] all in each of next 2 loops; end, ch 5, skip first 2 chs on ch-10 loop, 1 sc in each of next 6 chs. **Row 5**—Ch 10, turn, 1 sc in first loop, [ch 5, 1 sc] all in each of next 2 loops, ch 5, a Shell in next Shell, ch 5, skip first sc on Base of Pineapple, 1 sc in each of next 12 sc, ch 5, a Shell in next Shell. **Row 6**—Ch 5, turn, a Shell in first Shell, ch 5, skip first sc on Pineapple, 1 sc in each of next 10 sc, ch 5, a Shell in next Shell, [ch 5, 1 sc] all in each of next 3 loops; end as row 4. **Row 7**—Ch 10, turn, 1 sc in first loop, [ch 5, 1 sc] all in each of next 3 loops, ch 5, a Shell in next Shell, ch 5, skip first sc on Pineapple, 1 sc in

each of next 8 sc, ch 5, a Shell in next Shell. **Row 8**—Ch 5, turn, a Shell in first Shell, ch 5, skip first sc on Pineapple, 1 sc in each of next 6 sc, ch 5, a Shell in next Shell, [ch 5, 1 sc] all in each of next 4 loops; end as row 4. **Row 9**—Ch 10, turn, 1 sc in first loop, [ch 5, 1 sc] all in each of next 4 loops, ch 5, a Shell in next Shell, ch 5, skip first sc on Pineapple, 1 sc in each of next 4 sc, ch 5, a Shell in next Shell. **Row 10**—Ch 5, turn, a Shell in first Shell, ch 5, skip first sc on Pineapple, 1 sc in each of next 2 sc, ch 5, a Shell in next Shell, [ch 5, 1 sc] all in each of next 5 loops; end as row 4. **Row 11**—Ch 10, turn, 1 sc in first loop, [ch 5, 1 sc] all in each of next 5 loops, ch 5, a Shell in next Shell, skip the 2 sc on Pineapple, 1 sc in ch-2 sp of next Shell. **Row 12**—Ch 5, turn, a Shell in first Shell, ch 5, skip next loop, [1 dc, ch 6, 1 dc] all in next loop, ch 5, skip next loop, a Shell in next loop, 1 sc in next loop, ch 5, 1 sc in next loop; end as row 4. Rpt rows 3 to 12 inclusive for Pineapple pattern. Work the number of rpts as instructed for Doily, ending last rpt with row 10, then fasten off and tack together the centers of 2 Shells on last row. From wrong side sew lace into ring, matching Shells and loops.

SMALL ROUND DOILY—Work 19 patterns of Pineapple Lace Edging. To prepare linen circle, faintly draw a perfect circle 7 inches in diameter. Cut allowing ¼ in. all around. Sew Lace all around on faint line. Turn edge and sew ⅛-in. hem.

LARGE ROUND DOILY—Work 26 patterns of Pineapple Lace Edging. Prepare linen as for Small Round Doily only draw 11½ in. circle instead of 7.

OVAL DOILY—Work 26 patterns of Pineapple Lace Edging. To prepare linen, cut a paper circle 6½-ins. in diameter and cut circle across center. Paste half circles on another piece of paper so that center edges face each other 6 ins. apart. Place paper pattern on linen and faintly trace outline. Cut allowing ¼ in. all around. Sew Lace all around on faint line, easing in around curves. Turn edge and sew ⅛-in. hem.

Aloha Centerpiece

18 INCHES IN DIAMETER
Materials Required: AMERICAN THREAD COMPANY
"GEM" CROCHET COTTON, Article 35, size 30
2 balls White.   or
"STAR" CROCHET COTTON, Article 20, size 30
3 balls White.
Steel crochet hook No. 12.

Ch 10, join to form a ring, ch 4 and work 31 tr c in ring, join in 4th st of ch.

2nd Round. Ch 4 (always count as part of 1st cluster st at beginning of each round), 2 tr c in same space keeping last loop of each tr c on hook, thread over and work off all loops at one time, * ch 3, skip 1 tr c, cluster st in next tr c (cluster st: 3 tr c in same space keeping last loop of each tr c on hook, thread over and work off all loops at one time), repeat from * all around, ch 3, join in top of 1st cluster st.

3rd Round. Ch 4, cluster st in same space, * ch 2, tr c over next loop, ch 2, cluster st in next cluster st, repeat from * all around ending with ch 2, tr c over last loop, ch 2, join.

4th Round. Ch 4, cluster st in same space, * ch 3, tr c in next tr c, ch 3, cluster st in next cluster st, repeat from * all around ending with ch 3, tr c in next tr c, ch 3, join.

5th Round. Repeat 4th round but having ch 4 between cluster sts and tr c's.

6th Round. Repeat 4th round but having ch 5 between cluster sts and tr c's.

7th Round. Ch 4, cluster st in same space, ch 3, cluster st in same space (cluster st shell), * ch 4, tr c in next tr c, ch 4, cluster st shell in next cluster st, repeat from * all around ending with ch 4, tr c in next tr c, ch 4, join.

8th Round. Ch 4, cluster st in same space, * ch 5, cluster st in next cluster st of same cluster st shell, ch 3, tr c in next tr c, ch 3, cluster st in 1st cluster st of next cluster st shell, repeat from * all around ending to correspond, ch 3, join.

9th Round. Ch 4, cluster st in same space, * ch 9, cluster st in next cluster st, ch 3, tr c in next tr c, ch 3, cluster st in next cluster st, repeat from * all around ending to correspond, ch 3, join.

10th Round. Ch 4, cluster st in same space, ch 6, sl st in 6th st from hook for picot, * ch 13, s c in 6th st from hook to form picot, ch 7, cluster st in next cluster st, ch 6, sl st in 6th st from hook for picot, cluster st in next cluster st, repeat from * all around, ending to correspond, join.

11th Round. Sl st into picot, ch 4, cluster st shell in same picot, * ch 5, 6 tr c in next picot, ch 5, cluster st shell in next picot, repeat from * all around ending to correspond, ch 5, join. All shells are cluster st shells and will be referred to as shells for remainder of doily.

12th Round. Sl st into center of shell, ch 4, shell in same space, ** ch 5, s c in 1st tr c, * ch 6, s c in next tr c, repeat from * 4 times (pineapple), ch 5, shell in center of next shell, repeat from ** all around ending to correspond, ch 5, join.

13th Round. Sl st into shell, ch 4, shell in same space, ** ch 6, skip 1 loop, s c in 1st loop of pineapple, * ch 6, s c in next loop, repeat from * 3 times, ch 6, shell in next shell, repeat from ** all around ending to correspond, ch 6, join.

14th Round. Same as last round but having 3 loops across each pineapple.

15th Round. Sl st into shell, ch 4, shell in same space, ch 3, cluster st in same space, ** ch 6, s c in 1st loop of pineapple, * ch 6, s c in next loop, repeat from * once, ch 6, 3 cluster sts with ch 3 between each cluster st in center of next shell, repeat from ** all around ending to correspond, join.

16th Round. Sl st into shell, ch 4, shell in same space, * ch 9, s c in 6th st from hook for picot, ch 3, shell in next ch 3 loop, ch 6, s c in 1st loop of pineapple, ch 6, s c in next loop, ch 6, shell in next ch 3 loop, repeat from * all around ending to correspond, join.

17th Round. Sl st into shell, ch 4, shell in same space, * ch 5, 7 tr c in next picot, ch 5, shell in next shell, ch 6, s c in last loop of pineapple, ch 6, shell in next shell, repeat from * all around ending to correspond, join.

18th Round. Sl st into shell, ch 4, shell in same space, ** ch 5, s c in next tr c, * ch 6, s c in next tr c, repeat from * 5 times, ch 5, shell in next shell, ch 6, s c in next s c, ch 6, shell in next shell, repeat from ** all around ending to correspond, join.

19th Round. Sl st into shell, ch 4, shell in same space, ** ch 6, s c in 1st loop of pineapple, * ch 6, s c in next loop, repeat from * 4 times, ch 6, shell in next shell, shell in next shell, repeat from ** all around ending to correspond, join.

20th Round. Sl st into shell, ch 4, shell in same space, * ch 6, s c in 1st loop of pineapple, work 4-ch 6 loops across pineapple, ch 6, shell in next shell, ch 1, shell in next shell, repeat from * all around ending to correspond, join.

21st Round. Same as last round but having 3 loops across each pineapple and ch 2 between shells.

22nd Round. Sl st into shell, ch 4, shell in same space, ** ch 6, s c in 1st loop of pineapple, * ch 6, s c in next loop, repeat from * once, ch 6, shell in next shell, ch 9, s c in 6th st from hook for picot, ch 3, shell in next shell, repeat from ** all around ending to correspond, join.

23rd Round. Sl st into shell, ch 4, shell in same space, * ch 6, s c in 1st loop of pineapple, ch 6, s c in next loop, ch 6, shell in next shell, ch 6, 8 tr c in next picot, ch 6, shell in next shell, repeat from * all around ending to correspond, join.

24th Round. Sl st into shell, ch 4, shell in same space, ** ch 6, s c in last loop of pineapple, ch 6, shell in next shell, ch 6, s c in 1st tr c, * ch 6, s c in next tr c, repeat from * 6 times, ch 6, shell in next shell, repeat from ** all around ending to correspond, join.

25th Round. Sl st into shell, ch 4, shell in same space, ** ch 6, s c in next s c, ch 6, shell in next shell, ch 7, s c in 1st loop of pineapple, * ch 6, s c in next loop, repeat from * 5 times, ch 7, shell in next shell, repeat from ** all around ending to correspond, join.

26th Round. Sl st into shell, ch 4, shell in same space, * ch 2, shell in next shell, ch 8, s c in 1st loop of pineapple, then work 5-ch 6 loops across pineapple, ch 8, shell in next shell, repeat from * all around ending to correspond, join.

27th Round. Same as last round but having 4 loops across each pineapple and ch 4 between shells.

28th Round. Sl st into shell, ch 4, shell in same space, * ch 12, s c in 8th st from hook for picot, ch 4, shell in next shell, ch 8, s c in 1st loop of pineapple, work 3-ch 6 loops across pineapple, ch 8, shell in next shell, repeat from * all around ending to correspond, join.

29th Round. Sl st into shell, ch 4, shell in same space, * ch 4, 4 cluster sts with ch 2 between each cluster st in next picot, ch 4, shell in next shell, ch 8, s c in 1st loop of pineapple, work 2-ch 6 loops across pineapple, ch 8, shell in next shell, repeat from * all around ending to correspond, join.

30th Round. Sl st into shell, ch 4, shell in same space, ** ch 4, cluster st in next cluster st, * ch 2, tr c in next loop, ch 2, cluster st in next cluster st, repeat from * twice, ch 4, shell in next shell, ch 8, s c in 1st loop of pineapple, ch 6, s c in next loop, ch 8, shell in next shell, repeat from ** all around ending to correspond, join.

31st Round. Sl st into shell, ch 4, shell in same space, ** ch 4, cluster st in next cluster st, * ch 3, tr c in next tr c, ch 3, cluster st in next cluster st, repeat from * twice, ch 4, shell in next shell, ch 8, s c in remaining loop of pineapple, ch 8, shell in next shell, repeat from ** all around ending to correspond, join.

32nd Round. Sl st into shell, ch 4, shell in same space, ** ch 4, cluster st in next cluster st, * ch 4, tr c in next tr c, ch 4, cluster st in next cluster st, repeat from * twice, ch 4, shell in next shell, ch 8, s c in next s c, ch 8, shell in next shell, repeat from ** all around ending to correspond, join.

33rd Round. Sl st into shell, ch 4, shell in same space, ** ch 5, cluster st in next cluster st, * ch 5, tr c in next tr c, ch 5, cluster st in next cluster st, repeat from * twice, ch 5, shell in next shell, ch 3, shell in next shell, repeat from ** all around ending to correspond, join.

34th Round. Start of 1st point, sl st to center of shell, * ch 7, cluster st in next cluster st, ch 4, tr c in next tr c, ch 4, 2 tr c cluster st in next cluster st (2 tr c cluster st: 2 tr c in same space keeping last loop of each tr c on hook, thread over and work off all loops at one time), ** ch 4, turn, 1 tr c in same space, ch 3, tr c in next tr c, ch 3, 3 tr c cluster st in next cluster st, ch 4, turn, 2 tr c cluster st in same space, ch 2, tr c in next tr c, ch 2, 2 tr c cluster st in next 2 tr c cluster st, ch 4, turn, 1 tr c in same space, 3 tr c cluster st in next cluster st, ch 1, turn, sl st in top of cluster st just made, ch 6, sl st in same space for picot (top of point), ch 4 and working down side of point, sl st in base of the 2 tr c cluster st, * ch 4, sl st in base of next cluster st, repeat from * twice.

2nd Point. Ch 4 (counts as part of 1st cluster st), cluster st in same space as last sl st, ch 4, tr c in next tr c, ch 4, 2 tr c cluster st in next cluster st, repeat from ** to end of 1st point.

3rd Point. Work same as 2nd point finishing the picot at top of point, then ch 4 and working down side of point, sl st in base of 2 tr c cluster st, ch 4, sl st in base of next cluster st, ch 4, sl st in base of next cluster st, tr c in base of next cluster st, ch 7, s c in center of next shell of 33rd round, ch 4, tr c in loop at top of pineapple, ch 6, sl st in top of tr c just made for picot, tr c in same space, ch 4, s c in center of next shell, repeat from 1st * of 34th round 15 times, cut thread.

Pineapple Upside-Down Cake

MATERIALS: For centerpiece 17″ square: Daisy Mercerized Crochet Cotton, size 20, 1 skein or 2 balls; steel crochet hook No. 8.

FIRST MOTIF: Starting at center, ch 10. Join with sl st to form ring.

1st Rnd: Ch 4, holding back on hook the last loop of each tr, make 2 tr in ring, thread over and draw through all loops on hook (cluster made), * ch 9, holding back on hook the last loop of each tr, make 3 tr in ring, thread over and draw through all loops on hook (another cluster made). Repeat from * twice more; ch 9, sl st in top of first cluster.

2nd Rnd: Ch 4, complete cluster same as for first rnd, * ch 3, skip 4 ch, 7 tr in next ch, ch 3, cluster in next cluster. Repeat from * around, ending ch 3, sl st in top of first cluster.

3rd Rnd: Ch 4, complete cluster, * ch 3, tr in first tr, (ch 1, tr in next tr) 6 times; ch 3, cluster in next cluster. Repeat from * around. Join.

4th Rnd: Ch 4, complete cluster, ch 3, cluster in same place as first cluster, * ch 5, sc in first ch-1, (ch 3, sc in next ch-1) 5 times; ch 5, work cluster, ch 3 and cluster in next cluster. Repeat from * around. Join.

5th Rnd: Ch 4, complete cluster, * ch 3, skip next ch, cluster in next ch, ch 3, cluster in next cluster, ch 5, sc in first ch-3, (ch 3, sc in next ch-3) 4 times; ch 5, cluster in next cluster. Repeat from * around. Join.

6th Rnd: Ch 4, complete cluster, * ch 3, skip next ch, cluster in next ch, ch 3, work cluster, ch 3 and cluster in next cluster, ch 3, skip next ch, cluster in next ch, ch 3, cluster in next cluster, ch 5, sc in first ch-3, (ch 3, sc in next ch-3) 3 times; ch 5, cluster in next cluster. Repeat from * around. Join.

7th Rnd: Ch 4, complete cluster, * (ch 5, cluster in next cluster) 5 times; ch 5, sc in first ch-3, (ch 3, sc in next ch-3) twice; ch 5, cluster in next cluster. Repeat from * around. Join.

8th Rnd: Ch 4, complete cluster, * (ch 7, cluster in next cluster) 5 times; ch 5, sc in ch-3, ch 3, sc in next ch-3, ch 5, cluster in next cluster. Repeat from * around. Join.

9th Rnd: Ch 4, complete cluster, * (ch 9, cluster in next cluster) 5 times; ch 5, sc in ch-3, ch 5, cluster in next cluster. Repeat from * around. Join.

10th Rnd: Ch 4, complete cluster, * (ch 9, cluster in next cluster, ch 3, cluster in same cluster) 4 times; ch 9, cluster in each of next 2 clusters. Repeat from * around. Join and break off.

SECOND MOTIF: Work as for First Motif until 9 rnds are completed.

10th Rnd: Ch 4, complete cluster, (ch 9, cluster in next cluster, ch 3, cluster in same cluster) 3 times; ch 9, cluster in next cluster, ch 1, sc in corresponding ch-3 on first motif, ch 1, cluster in same cluster

EACH MOTIF 5 3/4″

as last cluster was made (joining made); ch 9, (cluster in next cluster) twice; ch 9, make another joining and complete rnd same as for First Motif. Make 3 rows of 3 motifs each, joining adjacent sides as second motif was joined to first motif.

Small Fill-in Motif: Attach thread to first cluster at tip of pineapple between 2 motifs. Ch 4, holding back last loop on hook, work tr in same cluster, 2 tr in next cluster, thread over and draw through all loops; then work 2 tr in each of the 2 clusters on opposite motif, complete as for cluster. Break off. Work remaining 11 fill-in motifs in same manner.

Large Fill-in Motif: Attach thread in ch-3 sp between 2 clusters following joining.

1st Rnd: Ch 4, complete cluster, ch 3, cluster in same sp, * ch 9, in next ch-3 between 2 clusters on same motif work cluster, ch 3 and cluster; in ch-3 on next motif work cluster, ch 3 and cluster. Repeat from * twice more; ch 9, cluster, ch 3 and cluster in next ch-3 sp. Join.

2nd Rnd: Sl st in next sp, ch 4, complete cluster, * ch 7, (cluster in next ch-3) twice. Repeat from * twice more; ch 7, cluster in next ch-3. Join.

3rd Rnd: Ch 4, complete cluster, (ch 2, cluster between next 2 clusters) 3 times; ch 2. Join and break off. Work remaining 3 fill-in motifs in same manner.

EDGING: Attach thread to last ch-3 preceding a joining, 2 sc in same sp, * ch 4, complete cluster making 3 tr in sp; ch 4, work a 3-tr cluster in 4th ch from hook, 2 sc in first ch-3 on next motif, 12 sc over each ch-9 and 4 sc over each ch-3 between 2 clusters to within next ch-3 sp preceding next joining; 2 sc in ch-3 sp. Repeat from * around. Join and break off. 🍮

Pineapple Sherbet Vanity Set

MATERIALS — DAISY Mercerized Crochet Cotton size 30:—3-balls or 2 skeins White, Cream or Ecru (sufficient for one large and 2 small doilies). Crochet hook size 13.

"PINEAPPLE SQUARE" — (Size—3¾")—Ch 12, sl st in 1st st. Ch 5, 4 tr in ring, (ch 7, 5 tr in ring) 3 times, ch 3, dc in top of 1st ch-5. **ROW 2**—Ch 8, turn, * sc in next tr, ch 2, dc in next 3 tr, ch 2, sl st in next (end) tr, ch 5, ** (dc, ch 7, dc) in center st of corner lp, ch 5. Repeat from * twice and from * to ** again. Dc in dc at end of last row, ch 3, dc in 3d st of next ch-8. **ROW 3**—Ch 5, turn, 5 tr over last ch-3, * tr in next dc, ch 7, sc in center dc of next petal, ch 7, tr in 1st dc at next corner, (6 tr, ch 2, 6 tr) all in corner ch-7. Repeat from * around. End with ch 2, sl st in top of 1st ch-5. **ROW 4**—Ch 10, turn, dc in next tr, * (ch 1, dc in next tr) 6 times, ch 6, dc in next tr, (ch 1, dc in next tr) 6 times, ch 7, dc in next tr. Repeat from * around. End with ch 1, sl st in 3d st of 1st ch-10. **ROW 5**—Ch 3, turn, dc in last ch-1 sp, * ch 3, sc in next sp, (ch 6, sc in next sp) 3 times, ch 3, holding back the last lp of each dc on hook, make 2 dc in next (end) sp, thread over and pull thru all lps on hook at once for a Cluster, ch 5, a 2-dc Cluster between 1st 2 dc on next pineapple, ch 3, sc in next sp, (ch 6, sc in next) 3 times, ch 3, a 2-dc Cluster in next (end) sp, ch 5, dc in corner lp, ch 5, a 2-dc Cluster between next 2 dc. Repeat from * around. End with ch 5, dc in corner lp, sk 1st ch-3, dc in next dc. **ROW 6**—Ch 1, turn, sk last dc, sl st in next (corner) dc, ch 8, * a 2-dc Cluster in next Cluster, ch 3, sc in next ch-6 lp, (ch 5, sc in next lp) twice, ch 3, a Cluster in next Cluster, ch 5, a Cluster in next Cluster, ch 3, sc in next ch-6 lp, (ch 5, sc in next lp) twice, ch 3, a Cluster in next Cluster, ch 5, (dc, ch 7, dc) in corner dc, ch 5 and repeat from * around. After final Cluster, ch 5, dc in corner dc in last row, ch 3, dc in 3d st of next ch-8. **ROW 7**—Ch 3, turn, 4 dc over last ch-3, * ch 6, a Cluster in next Cluster, ch 3, sc in next ch-5 lp, ch 5, sc in next lp, ch 3, a Cluster in next Cluster, ch 7, a Cluster in next Cluster, ch 3, sc in next ch-5 lp, ch 5, sc in next lp, ch 3, a Cluster in next Cluster, ch 6, (5 dc, ch 7, 5 dc) all in corner lp. Repeat from * around. End with 5 dc in corner sp, ch 3, dc in top of 1st ch-3. **ROW 8**—Ch 3, turn, 4 dc over last ch-3, * dc in next 3 dc, ch 10, a Cluster in next Cluster, ch 3, sc in next ch-5 lp, ch 3, a Cluster in next Cluster, ch 11, a Cluster in next Cluster, ch 3, sc in next ch-5 lp, ch 3, a Cluster in next Cluster, ch 10, sk 2 dc at cor-

ner, dc in next 3 dc, (5 dc, ch 7, 5 dc) in corner lp. Repeat from * around. End with 5 dc in corner lp, ch 3, dc in top of 1st ch-3. **ROW 9**—Ch 3, turn, (dc, ch 4, sl st in dc for a p, and 2 dc) all in corner sp, * dc in next dc, a p, dc in next 3 dc, a p, dc in next 2 dc, ch 13, a Cluster in next Cluster, ch 5, sl st in starting ch for a p, a Cluster in next Cluster, ch 14, a Cluster in next Cluster, ch 5, sl st in starting ch for a p, a Cluster in next Cluster, ch 13, sk first 2 dc at corner, (dc in next 3 dc, a p) twice, ** (3 dc, a p, 4 dc, a p and 2 dc) all in corner lp. Repeat from * around. End with (3 dc, a p, 2 dc) in corner lp, sl st in top of 1st ch-3. Cut 6" long, thread to a needle and fasten off on back.

2d SQUARE—Repeat to ** in Row 9. To join Squares, make (3 dc, a p and 4 dc) in corner lp, ch 2, sl st in opposite p on 1st Square, ch 2, sl st back in last dc to complete joining-p. Join the next 2 ps in same way to the next 2 opposite ps on 1st Square. After 3d p-joining, dc in next 2 dc, ch 13, a Cluster in next Cluster, * ch 3, sl st in opposite p on 1st Square, ch 2, sk last 2 sts of ch-3, sl st in next ch, a Cluster in next Cluster, * ch 14, a Cluster in next Cluster. Repeat from * to *. Join the 3 ps at next corner in same way as 1st 3 joining-ps, then complete row as for 1st Square. Continue to make and join Squares.

LARGE DOILY — (Size—15"x18¾")—Make 20 Squares and join 4x5.

SMALL DOILY — (Size — 7½"x 11¼")—Make 6 and join 2x3. Make a 2d Small Doily.

Stretch and pin doilies right-side-down in true shape, stretching several inches so all chains are taut. Steam and press dry thru a cloth.

Pineapples All in a Whirl Vanity Set

MATERIALS—DAISY Mercerized Crochet Cotton, size 30:—2-balls White, Cream or Ecru. Crochet hook size 12.
SMALL DOILY—(13″)—Ch 9, sl st in 1st st. Ch 3, 20 dc in ring, sl st in 1st 3-ch. **ROW 2**—Ch 6, 2 tr in same st, (3 tr in 1 lp of next dc) 7 times. **ROW 3**—Ch 7, turn, sk last tr, tr in next tr, (ch 1, tr in next tr) repeated across to end 6-ch. **ROW 4**—Ch 7, turn, tr in 1st 1-ch sp, (ch 2, tr in next sp) repeated across to end 7-ch. **ROW 5**—Ch 12, turn, sc in 1st 1-ch sp, (ch 6, sc in next sp) repeated across to end 7-ch. **ROW 6**—Ch 12, turn, sc in 1st 6-ch lp, (ch 6, sc in next lp) repeated across to end 6-ch lp. Repeat until point is worked out to one 6-ch lp. Ch 12, turn, sc in 6-ch lp. Fasten off. Make 4.

EDGE—With Row 1 of one pineapple right-side-up, join to Row 4, (2 sc, 2 hdc, 5 dc, 2 hdc and 2 sc) in 1st 12-ch lp on side of pineapple. * ch 2, (2 sc, 2 hdc, 5 dc, 2 hdc and 2 sc) in next 12-ch lp. Repeat from * around. Sc in end of Row 4, ch 21, sc in Row 4 on another pineapple, (2 sc, 2 hdc and 3 dc) in next 12-ch lp, sl st back in center of last shells on previous pineapple, (2 dc, 2 hdc and 2 sc) in bal. of 12-ch lp, ch 2 and join the next shell in same way to 2d shell on 1st pineapple. Repeat from * around for pineapple, joining final two and ending with the 21-ch lp. Fasten off.

CENTER—Ch 10, dc in 1st st, (ch 6, dc in same st) twice, **ch 6,** sl st in next 3d ch st. **ROW 2**—Ch 1, (7 sc in next sp,

1, sc in dc) 3 times, 7 sc in next sp, sl st in 1st 1-ch. **ROW 3**—Ch 5, a 2-tr-Cluster in same st, ch 5, a 3-tr-Cluster in same st, * (ch 4, a shell made of a 3-tr-Cluster, ch 5 and a 3-tr-Cluster worked in next 4th sc) 7 times, ch 4, sl st in 1st Cluster, sl st to 3d st of next 5-ch. **ROW 4**—Repeat last row to *. (Ch 8, a shell in center st of next shell) repeated around and join. Sl st to center st of 1st shell. **ROW 5**—Ch 5, a 2-tr-Cluster in same st, * ch 2, sl st in center st at base of one pineapple, ch 2 back and complete shell with a 3-tr-Cluster, ch 12, a Cluster in next shell, ch 3, sl st in next 21-ch lp between pineapples, ch 3 back and complete shell, ch 12, a Cluster in next shell. Repeat from * around until all pineapples have been joined. Join final **12-ch to 1st Cluster.** Fasten off.

BORDER—Join to 6th shell from joining of 2 pineapples, ch 5 for a tr, * (ch 11, tr in next shell) repeated around to 2d shell from next joining, ch 2, dtr in next shell, ch 2, dtr in 1st free shell on next pineapple, ch 2, tr in next. Repeat from * around and join to 5th st of 1st lp. **ROW 2** —* (6 sc, ch 5, sl st in last sc for a p, and 6 sc) in next 8 sps, (13 sc in next sp) 4 times, ** (2 sc in next sp) 3 times, 6 sc in next, ch 13, turn, sl st in 19th sc from hook, ch 1, turn, 15 sc in 13-ch, (6 sc in next sp) twice, turn, (ch 4, dtr in next 2d sc on center lp) 7 times, ch 4, sl st in center of next sp on edge, ch 1, turn, (2 sc, p, 2 sc) in each 4-ch sp, 1 sc in each dtr, (6 sc in next sp) twice, turn, (ch 8, dtr between next 2 ps) 7 times, ch 8, sl st in center of next sp on edge, ch 1, turn, (4 sc, p, 4 sc) in each 8-ch. 1 sc in each dtr. (6 sc in next sp) twice, turn, (ch 11, dtr between next 2 ps) 7 times, ch 11, sl st in center of next sp on edge, ch 1, turn, (6 sc, p, 6 sc) in each 11-ch, 1 sc in each dtr. 6 sc in next sp. ** Repeat from * around. Fasten off. Make 2.

LARGE DOILY—(15½″)—Ch 12, sl st in 1st st. Ch 6, 30 tr in ring, sl st in 6-ch. **ROW 2**—Ch 6, 2 tr in same st, (2 tr in next tr, 3 tr in next) 5 times, 2 tr in next tr. Repeat Rows 3, 4, 5 and 6 and complete pineapple. Make 4. Repeat Edge except join pineapples by 3 shells on each side. Repeat Center thru Row 4. **ROW 5**—Repeat Row 4 with 12-ch between shells. **ROW 6**—Repeat Row 5 of Small Doily Center except make 16-ch lps between shells.

BORDER—Join to 7th shell from joining of 2 pineapples, ch 5 for a tr and repeat Row 1 of Border beginning at *. **ROW 2**—(6 sc, p, 6 sc) in next 10 sps, (13 sc in next sp) 5 times. Repeat Row 2 of Border from ** to **. 6 sc in next sp, turn, (ch 15, dtr between ps) 7 times, ch 15, sl st in center of next sp on edge, ch 1, turn, (9 sc, p, 9 sc) in each 15-ch sp, 6 sc in next sp. Repeat from beginning of row.

Pin right-side-down in true circles, stretching several inches. Steam and press dry thru a cloth.

Mauna Loa Vanity Set

MATERIALS: J. & P. Coats *or* Clark's O.N.T. Best Six Cord Mercerized Crochet, *Size 30* . . . **Small Ball:** J. & P. Coats—*4 balls of White or Ecru,* or Clark's O.N.T.—*5 balls of White or Ecru.*

Oval Doily measures
10½ x 15 inches;
each Round Doily
9 inches in diameter.

OVAL DOILY—First Motif . . .
Starting at center, ch 10. Join with sl st to form ring. **1st rnd:** Ch 3, 23 dc in ring. Sl st in top of ch-3. **2nd rnd:** Ch 4, * dc in next dc, ch 1. Repeat from * around. Join last ch-1 to 3rd st of ch-4. **3rd rnd:** * Sc in next sp, ch 5. Repeat from * around, ending with sl st in first sc. Break off.

SECOND MOTIF . . . Work as for First Motif until 2nd rnd is completed. **3rd rnd:** * Sc in next sp, ch 5. Repeat from * until 6 loops are made, sc in

next sp (7 loops), ch 2, sl st in a loop of First Motif, ch 2, sc in next sp on Second Motif, ch 2, sl st in next loop on First Motif, ch 2, sc in next sp on Second Motif, and complete as for First Motif (no more joinings).

Make 3 more motifs same as this, joining 2 loops of each motif to 2 loops of previous motif, having 10 loops free on each side of joining.

Now work all around motifs as follows: **1st rnd:** Attach thread in 5th loop following joining on end motif, ch 4, tr in same loop, ch 5, skip 1 loop, (2 tr in next loop, ch 5) 10 times; skip next loop, 2 tr in next loop, ch 5, skip next loop, d tr in next loop, * d tr in 3rd free loop on next motif, ch 5, skip next loop, (2 t. in next loop, ch 5) twice; skip 1 loop, d tr in next loop. Repeat from * around, working over other end motif as before and joining last ch-5 to 4th ch of ch-4. **2nd rnd:** Sl st in next tr and in next 2 ch, sc in same loop, * ch 7, sc in next loop. Repeat from * around, ending with ch 7, sl st in first sc. **3rd rnd:**

Sl st in next 2 ch, sl st in loop, ch 4, holding back on hook the last loop of each tr make 2 tr in same loop, thread over and draw through all loops on hook (cluster); * ch 5, make a 3-tr cluster in next loop. Repeat from * around. Join last ch-5 with sl st to tip of first cluster. **4th rnd:** Sl st in next 2 ch, sc in loop, ch 5, in next loop make 2 dc, ch 2 and 2 dc (shell); * ch 5, shell in next loop. Repeat from * 5 more times; (ch 5, sc in next loop, ch 5, shell in next loop) 8 times; (ch 5, shell in next loop) 6 times; and complete rnd to correspond, ending with shell in last loop, ch 5. Sl st in first sc. Turn. **5th rnd:** Sl st in next 5 ch, in the next 2 dc and in sp of shell, turn, ch 3, in same sp make dc, ch 2 and 2 dc (shell over shell); * ch 5, in sp of next shell make 2 dc, ch 7 and 2 dc; ch 5, in sp of next shell make 2 dc, ch 2 and 2 dc (another shell over shell). Repeat from * around. Join. **6th rnd:** Sl st in next dc and in sp, * make shell over shell, 14 tr in next ch-7 loop. Repeat from *

(continued on page 26)

Round Pineapple Tablecloths

Materials for Large Round Tablecloth

J. & P. COATS KNIT-CRO-SHEEN

12 balls of White or Ecru, or 16 balls of any color.

Steel crochet hook No. 3.

Completed tablecloth measures about 72 inches in diameter.

irections . . . merely by a change of thread!

Materials for Small Round Tablecloth
CLARK'S O.N.T. or J. & P. COATS
BEST SIX CORD MERCERIZED CROCHET, size 30:

SMALL BALL:
CLARK'S O.N.T.—23 balls,
OR
J. & P. COATS —14 balls of White or Ecru, or 19 balls of any color.

BIG BALL:
J. & P. COATS—7 balls of White or Ecru, or 10 balls of any color.

Steel crochet hook No. 11. Completed tablecloth measures about 41 inches in diameter.

Directions:
Ch 15, join with sl st to form a ring. **1st rnd:** Ch 4, 43 tr in ring, sl st in top of ch-4. **2nd rnd:** Ch 5, make tr in each tr making ch 1 between tr's. Join last ch-1 with sl st to 4th st of starting ch. **3rd rnd:** Ch 6, make tr in each tr making ch 2 between tr's. Join as before. **4th rnd:** Sl st in next ch, sc in sp, ch 4, sc in next sp. Continue making ch-4 loops around, ending with ch 1, dc in 1st sc made. **5th, 6th and 7th rnds:** Ch 4, sc in next loop and continue making ch-4 loops around, ending with ch 1, dc in dc below. **8th rnd:** Sl st in loop, ch 4, tr in same loop, * ch 3, 2 tr in next loop. Repeat from * around. Join. **9th rnd:** Sl st in next tr and in

next sp, ch 3, in same sp make dc, ch 2 and 2 dc (shell made); in each sp around make a shell of 2 dc, ch 2 and 2 dc. Join with sl st to top of ch-3. **10th rnd:** Sl st in next dc and in next sp, ch 3 and complete a shell as before (shell over shell made), * ch 1, shell in sp of each of next 2 shells. Repeat from * around. Join. **11th rnd:** Sl st in next dc and in next sp, ch 3 and complete a shell as before, * ch 1, shell over next shell. Repeat from * around. Join. **12th rnd:** Make shell over shell increasing 1 ch in every other ch bar between shells. Join. **13th rnd:** Make shell over shell increasing 1 ch in all remaining ch bars (where no increases were made on previous rnd). Repeat 12th and

13th rnds alternately until 30th rnd is completed (there are 22 ch-11 bars and 22 ch-10 bars between shells on 30th rnd).

31st rnd: Sl st in next dc and in next sp, ch 3, dc in same sp, ch 5, 2 dc in same sp, * ch 11, shell over next shell, ch 11, in sp of next shell make 2 dc, ch 5 and 2 dc. Repeat from * around. Join. **32nd rnd:** Sl st in next dc and in next sp, ch 4, 14 tr in same sp—*this is base of pineapple;* * ch 7, shell over shell, ch 7, 15 tr in sp of next shell. Repeat from * around. Join. **33rd rnd:** Ch 5, make * tr in each tr, making ch 1 between tr's; ch 5, shell over shell, ch 5. Repeat from * around. Join to 4th st of ch-5. **34th rnd:** Sc in sp, * (ch 3, sc in

(continued overleaf)

next sp) 13 times; ch 5, shell over shell, ch 5, sc in next ch-1 sp. Repeat from * around. Join last ch-5 to 1st sc made. **35th rnd:** Sl st in next ch, sc in loop, * (ch 3, sc in next loop) 12 times; ch 5, shell over shell, ch 5, sc in next ch-3 loop. Repeat from * around. Join. **36th rnd:** Sl st in next ch, sc in loop, * (ch 3, sc in next loop) 11 times; ch 5, in sp of next shell make (2 dc, ch 2) twice and 2 dc; ch 5, sc in next ch-3 loop. Repeat from * around. Join. **37th rnd:** * Work 10 loops across pineapple, ch 5, shell in 1st ch-2 sp, ch 3, shell in next ch-2 sp, ch 5, sc in next ch-3 loop. Repeat from * around. Join. **38th rnd:** * Work 9 loops, ch 5, shell over shell, ch 1, shell in ch-3 sp—*this starts stem of 2nd rnd of pineapples;* ch 1, shell over next shell, ch 5, sc in next ch-3 loop. Repeat from * around. Join. **39th rnd:** * Work 8 loops, ch 5, shell over shell, (ch 2, shell over shell) twice; ch 5, sc in next loop. Repeat from * around. Join. **40th rnd:** * Work 7 loops, ch 5, shell over next shell, (ch 4, shell over next shell) twice; ch 5, sc in next loop. Repeat from * around. Join. **41st rnd:** * Work 6 loops, ch 5, shell over shell, ch 6, in sp of next shell make 2 dc, ch 5 and 2 dc; ch 6, shell over shell, ch 5, sc in next loop. Repeat from * around. Join. **42nd rnd:** * Work 5 loops, ch 5, shell over shell, ch 5, 15 tr in sp of next shell—*this is base of 2nd rnd of pineapples;* ch 5, shell in next shell, ch 5, sc in next loop. Repeat from * around. Join. **43rd rnd:** * Work 4 loops, ch 5, shell over shell, ch 5, tr in each tr making ch-1 between tr's, ch 5, shell over shell, ch 5, sc in next loop. Repeat from * around. **44th rnd:** * Work 3 ch-3 loops, ch 5, shell over shell, ch 5, sc in 1st ch-1 sp, (ch 4, sc in next sp) 13 times; ch 5, shell over shell, ch 5, sc in next loop. Repeat from * around. Join. **45th rnd:** * Work 2 ch-3 loops, ch 5, shell over shell, ch 5, sc in next loop, make 12 ch-4 loops, ch 5, shell over shell, ch 5, sc in next loop. Repeat from * around. Join. **46th rnd:** * Work 1 ch-3 loop, ch 5, shell over shell, ch 5, sc in next ch-4 loop, make 11 ch-4 loops, ch 5, shell over shell, ch 5, sc in next loop. Repeat from * around. Join.

47th rnd: Sl st in next ch, sc in loop, * ch 5, shell over shell, ch 5, sc in next ch-4 loop, make 10 ch-4 loops—*hereafter all loops on pineapples will be ch-4 loops;* ch 5, shell over shell, ch 5, sc in next loop. Repeat from * around. Join. **48th rnd:** Ch 5, * shell over shell, ch 5, work across pineapple, ch 5, shell over shell, ch 1, tr in next sc, ch 1. Repeat from * around. Join last ch-1 to 4th st of ch-5. **49th rnd:** Ch 3, in same place as sl st make dc, ch 2 and 2 dc (shell made)—*this starts stem of 3rd rnd of pineapples;* ch 2, * shell over shell, work across pineapple, shell over shell, ch 2, shell in tr, ch 2. Repeat from * around. Join. **50th rnd:** Sl st in next dc and in next sp, ch 3 and complete shell as before, ch 3, shell over shell, * work across pineapple, shell over shell, (ch 3, shell over shell) twice. Repeat from * around. Join. **51st rnd:** Shell over shell, ch 5, shell over shell and continue in pattern around. Join. **52nd rnd:** Sl st to sp, ch 3, dc in same sp, ch 5, 2 dc in same sp, * ch 7, shell over shell and continue in pattern around. Join. **53rd rnd:** Sl st to sp, ch 4, 17 tr in same sp—*this is base of 3rd rnd of pineapples;* * ch 5, shell over shell,

work across pineapple, shell over shell, ch 5, 18 tr in loop of next shell. Repeat from * around. Join.

Work in pattern as established, working stem for 4th rnd of pineapples exactly as stem for 3rd rnd of pineapples until 3rd rnd of stem is completed. **Next rnd:** Work across pineapple, shell over shell, (ch 7, shell over shell) twice; and continue in pattern around. **Following rnd:** Work across pineapple, shell over shell, ch 9, in sp of next shell make 2 dc, ch 5 and 2 dc; ch 9, shell over shell and continue in pattern around. **Next rnd:** Work 21 tr for base of each pineapple of 4th rnd of pineapples.

Continue in pattern as before until 4th rnd of stem of next (5th) rnd of pineapples is completed. **Next rnd:** Same as previous rnd but working ch 9 on each side of stem shell. **Following rnd:** Sl st to sp, ch 4, tr in same sp, ch 7, 2 tr in same sp, * ch 7, shell over shell, work across pineapple, shell over shell, in sp of next shell work 2 tr, ch 7 and 2 tr. Repeat from * around. Join. **Next rnd:** Sl st to sp, ch 5, 23 d tr in same sp, ch 5, shell over shell and continue in pattern around, making 24 d tr for base of each pineapple of 5th rnd of pineapples. Join. **Following rnd:** Ch 6, make d tr in each d tr with ch 1 between d tr's, ch 5 and continue in pattern around. Join to 5th st of ch-6.

Continue in pattern, working 6th rnd of pineapples exactly the same as 5th rnd of pineapples until 2nd rnd of d tr's at base of 6th rnd of pineapples is completed. Now continue to work ch-4 loops as before on 5th pineapple but work ch-5 loops on 6th pineapple until 5th pineapple is completed (there are 14 loops on each pineapple of 6th rnd).

To make points, sl st to sp of next shell and work in rows over each pineapple separately as follows: **1st row:** Ch 3 and complete shell as before, work across pineapple, shell over shell, ch 5, turn. **2nd row:** Shell over shell, ch 5, work across pineapple, shell over shell, ch 5, turn. Repeat the 2nd row until 1 loop remains on pineapple. Ch 5, turn. **Next row:** Shell over shell, ch 4, sc in loop, ch 4, 2 dc in next shell, ch 1, sl st back in ch-2 of last shell, ch 1, 2 dc where last 2 dc were made. Fasten off. Attach thread to sp of shell on next pineapple; complete point in same manner. Continue thus until all points have been completed.

Work 2 rnds all around tablecloth as follows: **1st rnd:** Attach thread to tip of one point where shells were joined, ch 3, at base of ch-3 make dc, ch 2 and 2 dc. * (Ch 3, shell in next turning ch between 2 rows) 7 times; ch 2, then holding back on hook the last loop of each dc, work dc in sp of next shell (on last complete rnd of tablecloth) and dc in sp of next shell (where thread was attached to work next point); thread over and draw through all loops on hook, (ch 3, shell in turning ch between 2 rows) 7 times; ch 3, shell at tip of next point where shells were joined. Repeat from * around. Join last ch-3 to top of starting ch. **2nd rnd:** Sl st in next dc and in next sp, ch 8, sc in 5th ch from hook (p made). Dc in same place as sl st, * ch 3, sc under next ch-3, ch 3, in next shell make dc, p and dc. Repeat from * 6 more times; ch 3, sc in tip of joined dc's, ch 3, in next shell make dc, p and dc. Ch 3, sc under next ch-3. Continue thus around. Fasten off. ☙

Mauna Loa Vanity Set
(continued from page 23)

around. Join. **7th rnd:** * Shell over shell, (tr in next tr, ch 1) 13 times; tr in next tr. Repeat from * around. Join. **8th rnd:** Sl st in next dc and in sp, ch 3, in same sp make dc, (ch 2, 2 dc) twice; * ch 1, sc in next ch-1 sp, (ch 3, sc in next ch-1 sp) 12 times; ch 1, in sp of next shell make 2 dc, (ch 2, 2 dc) twice. Repeat from * around. Join. **9th rnd:** Sl st in next dc and in next sp, ch 3 and complete shell in same sp as before, * shell in next ch-2 sp, ch 2, sc in next ch-3 loop, (ch 3, sc in next loop) 11 times; ch 2, shell in next ch-2 sp. Repeat from * around. Join. **10th rnd:** * Shell over shell, ch 3, shell over shell, ch 4, sc in next ch-3 loop, (ch 3, sc in next loop) 10 times; ch 4. Repeat from * around. Join.

Now work pineapples individually as follows: **1st row:** Sl st to sp of 2nd shell, ch 3 and complete shell in same sp as before, ch 4, sc in next ch-3 loop, (ch 3, sc in next loop) 9 times; ch 4, shell over shell. Ch 5, turn. **2nd row:** Shell over shell, ch 4, sc in next ch-3 loop, (ch 3, sc in next loop) 8 times; ch 4, shell over shell. Ch 5, turn. Continue in this manner, having one ch-3 loop less on each row until one loop remains. **Next row:** Shell over shell, ch 4, sc in next ch-3 loop, ch 4, shell over shell. Ch 5, turn, (shell over shell) twice. Break off.

Attach thread to sp of next free shell on 10th rnd and work next pineapple as before. Work all pineapples in this manner.

ROUND DOILY (Make 2)—Center Motif . . . Starting at center, ch 12. Join with sl st to form ring. **1st rnd:** Ch 3, 27 dc in ring. Join. **2nd and 3rd rnds:** Repeat 2nd and 3rd rnds of Motifs of Oval Doily. **4th rnd:** Sl st in next ch, sl st in loop, ch 4, tr in same loop, * ch 5, skip next loop, 2 tr in next loop. Repeat from * around Join. **5th rnd:** Repeat 2nd rnd of Oval Doily. **6th rnd:** Repeat 3rd rnd of Oval Doily, making ch 8 (instead of ch-5) between clusters. **7th rnd:** Sl st in next ch and in loop, ch 3, in same loop make dc, ch 2 and 2 dc (shell); * ch 5, shell in next loop. Repeat from * around. Join. **8th rnd:** * Make shell over shell, ch 6, in sp of next shell make 2 dc, ch 7 and 2 dc; ch 6. Repeat from * around. Join. **9th to 13th rnds incl:** Repeat 6th to 10th rnds incl of Oval Doily.

Complete pineapples individually as for Oval Doily. ☙

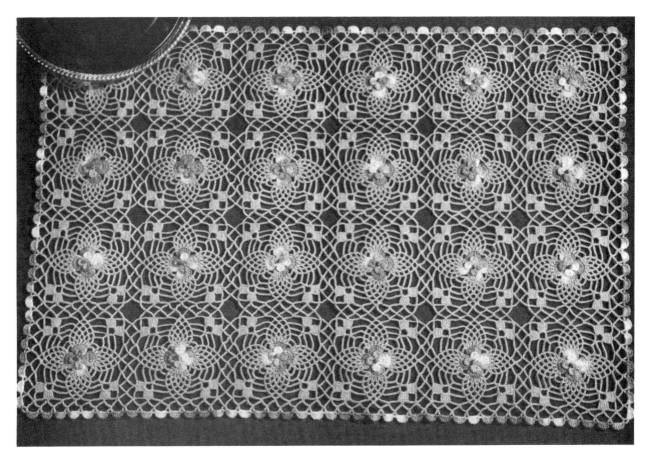

Pineapple Placemat

Shown in color on the inside front cover.

Materials

Materials	Quantity	Approx. Size of Motif	Size of Crochet Hook
"DAISY" Mercerized Crochet Cotton Art. 65, Size 20 or 30 **or**	1 skein Shd. Yellows will make 37 or 50 Motifs and 1 skein Lt. Green will make 20 or 26 Motifs	3 or 2¾ inches	Steel 12 or 13
"DAISY" Mercerized Crochet Cotton Art. 97, Size 30 **or**	1 ball Shd. Yellows will make 31 Motifs and 1 ball Lt. Green will make 16 Motifs	2¾ inches	Steel 13
"MERCROCHET" Cotton, Art. 161, Size 20 or 30 **or**	1 ball Shd. Yellows will make 25 or 31 Motifs and 1 ball Bright Nile Green will make 13 or 16 Motifs	3 or 2¾ inches	Steel 12 or 13
"SKYTONE" Mercerized Crochet Cotton Art. 123 **and**	1 ball Shd. Yellows will make 13 Motifs and 1 ball Lt. Green will make 8 Motifs	4½ inches	Steel 10
1 skein Lily Six Strand Floss, No. 181 — Spring Green.			

MOTIF—Starting in center with Shd. Yellows ch 8, join with sl st to form ring.

1st rnd—Ch 1, 12 sc in ring, join with sl st in back lp of 1st sc.

2d rnd—* Ch 4 and working in back lps around ring, 2 tr in same sc, 3 dtr in next sc, 2 tr in next sc, ch 4, sl st in same sc, sl st in next sc. Repeat from * around (4 petals). Cut 6 inches long, thread to a needle and fasten off on back.

3d rnd—Join Lt. Green to last tr on left side of 1 petal, * ch 5, sc in 1st tr on next petal, (ch 5, sc in next st) 6 times. Repeat from * around, ending with ch 2 and dc in place of final ch-5 lp (28 lps).

4th rnd—* Ch 6, sk lp between petals, sc in 1st lp on next petal, (ch 5, sc in next lp) 5 times. Repeat from * around, ending with ch 2, dc in dc at end of last rnd. for final lp.

5th rnd—* Ch 10, sc in 1st ch-5 lp on next petal, (ch 5, sc in next lp) 4 times. Repeat from * around, ending as in last rnd.

6th rnd—* Ch 8, dc in center of next ch-10 lp, ch 8, sc in next ch-5 lp, (ch 5, sc in next lp) 3 times. Repeat from * around, ending as in 4th rnd.

7th rnd—* Ch 10, (dc, ch 7, dc) in next dc, ch 10, sc in next ch-5 lp, (ch 5, sc in next lp) twice. Repeat from * around, ending as in 4th rnd.

8th rnd—* Ch 11, in corner ch-7 sp make 5 tr, ch 9 and 5 tr; ch 11, sc in next ch-5 lp, ch 5, sc in next lp. Repeat from * around, ending as in 4th rnd.

9th rnd—* Ch 10, sc in middle of next ch-11 lp, ch 10, sk 2

(continued on page 48)

Rising Sun Tablecloth

**MATERIALS: CLARK'S O.N.T. or J. & P. COATS
BEST SIX CORD MERCERIZED CROCHET, size 30:**

SMALL BALL:
CLARK'S O.N.T.—79 balls,
OR
J. & P. COATS —49 balls.

BIG BALL:
J. & P. COATS—25 balls.

Steel crochet hook No. 10 or 11.

GAUGE: Each motif measures about 4½ inches in diameter after blocking. For a tablecloth about 63 x 81 inches, make 252 motifs.

FIRST MOTIF . . . Ch 8. Join with sl st to form ring. **1st rnd:** Ch 4 (to count as tr), 23 tr in ring. Join with sl st to top st of 1st ch-4. **2nd rnd:** Ch 7 (to count as tr and ch-3), tr in same place as sl st, * ch 4, skip 2 tr, in next tr make tr, ch 3 and tr. Repeat from * around, joining last ch-4 to 4th st of 1st ch-7. **3rd rnd:** Sl st in next sp, ch 3, in same sp make dc, ch 3 and 2 dc; * ch 4, in next sp make 2 dc, ch 3 and 2 dc. Repeat from * around. Join. **4th rnd:** Sl st to next sp, ch 3, 6 dc in same sp, * ch 3, skip next sp, 7 dc in next sp (between dc groups). Repeat from * around. Join. **5th rnd:** Ch 4, dc in next dc, (ch 1, dc in next dc) 5 times; * ch 4, dc in next 7 dc with ch-1 between. Repeat from * around. Join to 3rd st of 1st ch. **6th rnd:** Sl st in next ch-1 sp, ch 1, sc in same sp, (ch 5, sc in next sp) 5 times; * ch 7, sc in next ch-1 sp, (ch 5, sc in next sp) 5 times. Repeat from * around. Join last ch-7 to 1st sc. **7th rnd:** Sl st to center of next loop, ch 1, sc in same loop, * (ch 5, sc in next loop) 4 times; ch 3, in center st of chain below make 6 dc, ch 3, sc in next loop. Repeat from * around. Join. **8th rnd:** Sl st to center of next loop, ch 1, sc in same loop, * (ch 5, sc in next loop) 3 times; ch 3, dc in next 6 dc with ch-1 between, ch 3, skip next sp, sc in next loop. Repeat from * around. Join. **9th rnd:** Sl st to center of next loop, ch 1, sc in same loop, * (ch 5, sc in next loop) twice; ch 4, sc in next ch-1 sp, (ch 5, sc in next sp) 4 times; ch 4, sc in next loop. Repeat from * around. Join. **10th rnd:** Sl st to center of next loop, ch 1, sc in same loop, * ch 5, sc in next loop, ch 5, skip next sp, sc in next loop, (ch 5, sc in next loop) 3 times; ch 5, sc in next loop. Repeat from * around. Join. **11th rnd:** Sl st to center of next loop, ch 1, sc in same loop, * ch 8, skip next sp, sc in next loop, (ch 5, sc in next loop)

twice; ch 8, skip next sp, sc in next loop. Repeat from * around. Join. **12th rnd:** Ch 1, sc in same place as sl st, * ch 11, skip next sp, sc in next loop, ch 5, sc in next loop, ch 11, sc in next sc. Repeat from * around. Join and fasten off.

SECOND MOTIF . . . Work as for 1st motif until 11th rnd is complete. **12th rnd:** Ch 1, sc in same place as sl st, ch 5, drop loop from hook, insert hook in center st of corresponding ch-11 on 1st motif and pull dropped loop through, ch 5, sc in next loop on 2nd motif, ch 2, drop loop from hook, insert hook in center st on corresponding loop of 1st motif and pull loop through, ch 2, sc in next loop on 2nd motif, ch 5, drop loop from hook, insert hook in center st on next ch-11 on 1st motif and pull dropped loop through, ch 5, sc in next sc on 2nd motif. Now complete rnd as for 1st motif (no more joinings). Make 14 x 18 motifs joining them as 2nd motif was joined to 1st, having 1 small pineapple free between joinings.

FILL-IN-MOTIF . . . Ch 6. Join with sl st to form ring. **1st rnd:** Ch 1, sc in ring, (ch 5, sc in ring) 3 times; ch 3. Join. **2nd rnd:** Sl st to center of next loop, ch 3, 4 dc in same loop, ch 2, 5 dc in next loop. Repeat from * around. Join. **3rd rnd:** Ch 4, dc in next dc, (ch 1, dc in next dc) 3 times; * ch 3, dc in next 5 dc with ch-1 between. Repeat from * around. Join. **4th rnd:** Sl st

in next ch-1 sp, ch 1, sc in same sp, * (ch 5, sc in next sp) 3 times; ch 6, sc in next ch-1 sp. Repeat from * around. Join. **5th rnd:** Sl st to center of next loop, * (ch 5, sc in next loop) twice; ch 10, sc in next ch-5 loop. Repeat from * around. Join. **6th rnd:** Sl st to center of next loop, ch 1, sc in same loop, ch 7, sc in next loop, ch 7, join to 4th st of a free ch-11 between motifs, * ch 7, sc under the next ch-10 of Fill-in-motif, ch 7, join to corresponding st on next ch-11 on motif, ch 7, sc in next loop on Fill-in-motif, ch 7, sc in next loop on Fill-in-motif, ch 7, join as before to next free ch-11 between motifs. Repeat from * around. Join and fasten off. Work Fill-in-motifs in this manner in all sps between motifs.

EDGING . . . Attach thread to outer edge, in each ch-11 loop around make sc, h dc, 4 dc, 5 tr, 4 dc, h dc, sc; in each short chain at joinings make 7 sc. Fasten off.

Polynesian Dinner

"PINEAPPLE" MOTIF

Each motif measures appx. 5¾", edge 2½" wide.

DINNER CLOTH SIZES			BEDSPREAD SIZES		
Appx. Size	Motifs	Rows	Appx. Size	Mo'ifs	Rows
62½" x 62½"	100	10 wide / 10 long	Twin Size		
			74" x 108½"	216	12 wide / 18 long
62½ x 85½	140	10 wide / 14 long			
			Double Size		
85½" x 102¾"	238	14 wide / 17 long	91¼" x 108½"	270	15 wide / 18 long

Cloth or Bedspread

How To Choose Your Thread

The thread you choose will determine the size of your crocheted motif. You may vary the size of your project by changing the size of your thread. This tablecloth was made with a size 18 soft finish cotton crochet thread. Choose your thread, crochet up one entire ball, skein or cone, and this will give you the correct size of one motif and the amount of motifs obtained from one unit. Then it will be simple for you to estimate how much more thread you will need to complete your project.

Large Motif

1st Row: Chain 8 and join with a slip stitch to form a ring — ch 3 (for 1st double crochet) — 23 more d c in ring (total of 24 d c).

2nd Row: Ch 4 — 1 d c in same st — * ch 4 — skip 2 d c — 1 d c in next st — ch 1 — 1 more d c in same st, repeat from * around joining last ch 4 to 3rd st of 1st ch 4 (total of 8 groups of 2 d c each with ch 4 between each group), sl st to ch 1 of 1st group.

3rd Row: 1 shell over ch 1 made thus — ch 3 — 1 d c over ch 1 — ch 4 — 2 more d c over same ch 1 — * 1 shell over ch 1 of next group, repeat from * around, join and sl st to 1st ch 4 which is center of shell.

4th Row: Sh over 1st ch 4 thus — ch 3 — 2 d c over ch 4 — ch 3 — 3 more d c over same ch 4 — * 9 treble crochet (thread twice over the hook) over next ch 4 — 1 sh over next ch 4, repeat from * around, join and sl st to center of sh.

5th Row: Sh over sh (made like sh in 4th row) — * ch 3 — sl st to top of 1st tr c — ch 5 — sl st to top of next tr c, repeat until there are 8 loops — ch 3 — sh over next sh, repeat from * around, join and sl st to center of sh.

6th Row: Sh made thus — ch 3 — 3 more d c in same space — ch 2 — 4 more d c in same sp — ch 2 — 4 more d c in same sp — * ch 3 — sl st over 1st loop of pineapple — ch 5 — sl st over next loop, repeat until there are 7 loops — ch 3 — sh over next sh, repeat from * around, join and sl st to 1st ch 2 of 1st sh.

7th Row: Sh made thus — ch 3 — 3 more d c in same sp — ch 3 — 4 more d c in same sp — ch 2 — sh over next ch 2 — * ch 3 — sl st to 1st loop — ch 5 — sl st to next loop, repeat until there are 6 loops — ch 3 — sh over next sh, repeat from * around, join and sl st to center of sh.

8th Row: * Sh over sh — ch 2 — 1 filet block (of 4 d c) over ch 2 between sh of preceding row — ch 2 — sh over next sh — ch 3 — sl st to 1st loop — ch 5 — sl st to next loop, repeat until there are 5 loops — ch 3, repeat from * around join and sl st to center of sh.

9th Row: * Sh over sh — ch 2 — 3 blocks (10 d c) — ch 2 — sh over next sh — ch 3 — sl st to 1st loop — ch 5 — sl st to next loop, repeat until there are 4 loops — ch 3, repeat from * around, join and sl st to center of sh.

10th Row: * Sh over sh — ch 2 — 5 blocks (16 d c) — ch 2 — sh over next sh — ch 4 — 3 loops — ch 4, repeat from * around, join and sl st to center of sh.

11th Row: * Sh over sh — ch 2 — 7 blocks (22 d c) — ch 2 — sh over next sh — ch 6 — 2 loops — ch 6, repeat from * around, join and sl st to center of sh.

12th Row: * Sh over sh — ch 2 — 9 blocks (28 d c) — ch 2 — sh over next sh — ch 8 — 1 loop — ch 8, repeat from * around, join and sl st to center of sh.

13th Row: * Sh over sh — ch 2 — 11 blocks (34 d c) — ch 2 — sh over next sh — ch 10 — sl st to center of last loop — ch 10, repeat from * around, join and fasten off.

Make the required number of Pineapple motifs and sew together at sides being very careful to match sh to sh and block to block, thus forming a diamond, then make the small motifs by which the large motifs are joined at corners.

Small Motif

1st Row: Ch 6 and join to form ring — ch 2 (for 1st single crochet) — 15 more s c in ring (total of 16 s c).

2nd Row: Ch 4 (for 1st treble crochet) — 1 more tr c in same st — * ch 5 — skip 1 st — 2 tr c in next st, repeat from * around, joining last ch 5 to top of 1st tr c (total of 8 groups of 2 tr c each), sl st to center of 1st group.

3rd Row: Ch 3 — 1 more d c in same sp — ch 3 — 2 more d c in same sp — * ch 1 — 1 sh between next 2 tr c, repeat from * around, joining last ch 1 to top of 1st ch 3, sl st to center of sh.

4th Row: Ch 3 — 3 more d c in same sp — * ch 2 — sl st to center of joining of two of the large motifs — ch 2 — 4 more d c in same sp with the 1st 4 d c thus completing a sh and fasten with sl st over the ch 1 of preceding row — sl st to center of next sh and ch 6 — fasten with sl st to end of ch 10 of large motifs — ch 6 and sl st over center of same sh — ch 10 and fasten with sl st over center of last loop of pineapple — ch 10 and again sl st over 3 of sh — ch 6 and fasten with sl st to end of other ch 10 of large motif — ch 6 and again sl st over 3 of sh — sl st to next ch 1 of preceding row — 4 d c over center of next sh, repeat from * around, fasten off.

Crochet Edge

1st Row: First complete each diamond (all around edge) thus, attach thread in last d c of sh and ch 3 — 2 d c over ch 2 — 1 d c in next d c — ch 2 — skip 2 d c, and work 9 blocks (28 d c) — ch 2 — 1 bl (4 d c) over last sp of diamond, turn work and sl st back to open sp.

2nd Row: 1 bl over open sp — ch 2 — skip 2 d c — 7 bl (22 d c) — 1 sp — 1 bl, turn work and sl st back to open sp, always do this at end of row.

3rd Row: 1 bl — 1 sp — 5 bl (16 d c) — 1 sp — 1 bl.

4th Row: 1 bl — 1 sp — 3 bl (10 d c) — 1 sp — 1 bl.

5th Row: 1 bl — 1 sp — 1 bl (4 d c) — 1 sp — 1 bl.

6th Row: 1 bl — 1 sp — 1 bl.

7th Row: 1 bl, fasten off.

Now starting at second diamond from a corner and working towards corner, attach thread to top of 1st ch 3 of 1st bl of 1st row and * ch 5 — sl st to corner of next bl, repeat until you come down to point of diamond — ch 8, sl st to other corner of bl, then continue up other side of diamond, * sl st last ch 5 to center of sh — ch 5 — 1 d c in 4th d c of sh — ch 15 and sl st over last loop of pineapple — ch 15 — 1 d c in 4th d c of other sh — ch 5 — sl st to center of sh (which will be the joining of the two motifs) — ch 5 — 1 d c in 4th d c of next sh — ch 15 and sl st over last loop of next pineapple — ch 15 — 1 d c in 4th d c of next sh — ch 5 — sl st to center of shell — ch 5 then continue down side of diamond, around point and up other side, and repeat from * all around.

2nd Row: 1 row of filet sp all around working thus at pineapple points — ch 5, and sl st to 3rd st of the ch 15 — ch 5, and sl st to the corresponding 3rd st of the other ch 15, then continue, ch 5, and sl st to next ch 5.

3rd Row: 1 row of filet sp all around.

4th Row: 1 row of filet sp all around.

5th Row: Starting at sp at point of diamond — ch 3 — 3 more d c in same sp — ch 3 — 4 more d c — ch 3 — 4 more d c all in same sp — * skip next ch 5 — sh over next ch 5 thus, 4 d c — ch 3 — 4 d c, repeat from * all around.

Hawaiian Luncheon Set

MATERIALS: J. & P. Coats *or* Clark's O.N.T. Best Six Cord Mercerized Crochet, *Size 30* . . . **Small Ball:** J. & P. Coats—*4 balls of White or Ecru, or 5 balls of any color, or* Clark's O.N.T.—*7 balls of White or Ecru, or 8 balls of any color* . . . *Steel Crochet Hook No. 10.*

Centerpiece measures 15½ inches in diameter; Place Doily 11½ inches in diameter and Glass Doily 7½ inches in diameter.

CENTERPIECE . . . Starting at center, ch 8. Join. **1st rnd:** Ch 3, 27 dc in ring. Sl st in 3rd st of ch-3. **2nd rnd:** Sc in same place as sl st, * ch 3, skip 1 dc, sc in next dc. Repeat from * around, ending with ch 3, sl st in first sc. **3rd rnd:** Sl st to center of next loop, sc in same loop, * ch 4, sc in next loop. Repeat from * around, ending with ch 4, sl st in first sc. **4th to 8th rnds incl:** Continue making chain loops, having 1 additional chain on each loop of each rnd (ch-9 loops on 8th rnd). **9th rnd:** Repeat 8th rnd. **10th rnd:** Sl st in next loop, ch 3, 8 dc in first loop, 9 dc in each loop around. Join. **11th rnd:** Sc in same place as sl st, * ch 3, skip 2 dc, sc in next dc. Repeat from * around, ending with sl st in first sc (42 loops). **12th rnd:** Sl st in last loop made, ch 3, dc in next loop, ch 3, dc in top of dc (picot), dc in same loop, * dc in next loop, ch 3, dc in top of dc (another picot), dc in same loop. Repeat from * around, ending with dc in last loop, picot, sl st in top of ch-3. **13th rnd:** Ch 6, dc in 4th ch from hook (picot), dc in next dc, * ch 1, dc in next dc, picot, dc in next dc. Repeat from * around. Join. **14th rnd:** Ch 4, * in next ch-1 sp make dc, picot and dc; ch 1. Repeat from * around, ending with picot, sl st in 3rd st of ch-4. **15th rnd:** Sl st in next ch, ch 6, dc in 4th ch from hook, dc in base of ch-6, * ch 3, in next ch-1 make dc, picot and dc. Repeat from * around, ending with ch 3, sl st in 3rd st of

ch-6. **16th rnd:** Sl st to center ch of next ch-3, ch 6, picot, dc at base of ch-6, * ch 3, in center st of next ch-3 make dc, picot and dc. Repeat from * around. Join as before. Work in this manner in established pattern, having ch 5 (instead of ch-3) for the next 2 rnds, ch 7 for the following 2 rnds and ch 9 on the next rnd, ending each rnd with sl st in 3rd st of ch-6. **22nd rnd:** Sl st to center ch of next chain, ch 3, in same place make dc, ch 2 and 2 dc (shell); * ch 5, in center ch of next chain make 2 dc, ch 6 and 2 dc; ch 5, in center ch of next chain make 2 dc, ch 2 and 2 dc (another shell). Repeat from * around. Join. **23rd rnd:** Sl st in next dc and in sp of shell, ch 3, in same sp make dc, (ch 2, 2 dc) twice; * ch 1, 10 tr in next ch-6 sp, ch 1, in ch-2 sp of next shell make 2 dc, (ch 2, 2 dc) twice. Repeat from * around. Join. **24th rnd:** Sl st in next dc and in ch-2 sp, ch 3 and complete shell in same sp, * ch 1, shell in next sp, ch 1, (tr in next tr, ch 1) 10 times; shell in next ch-2 sp. Repeat from * around. Join. **25th rnd:** Sl st in next dc and in sp, ch 3 and complete shell as before, * ch 3, shell in sp of next shell, ch 2, skip next sp, sc in next ch-1 sp between tr's, (ch 3, sc in next sp) 8 times; ch 2, shell in sp of next shell. Repeat from * around. Join.

Now complete pineapples individually as follows: **1st row:** Sl st in next dc and in sp of shell, turn. Ch 5, shell over shell, ch 4, skip ch-2, sc in next ch-3 loop, (ch 3, sc in next loop) 7 times; ch 4, shell over shell. Ch 5, turn. **2nd row:** Shell over shell, ch 4, sc in next ch-3 loop, (ch 3, sc in next loop) 6 times; ch 4, shell over shell. Ch 5, turn. Work in this manner until one ch-3 loop remains. Ch 5, turn. **Next row:** Shell over shell, ch 4, sc in ch-3 loop, ch 4, shell over shell, ch 5, turn, (shell over shell) twice. Break off. Attach thread to sp of next free shell, make shell over shell and complete pineapple as before. Work all pineapples in this manner.

EDGING . . . **1st rnd:** Attach thread in ch-3 sp at base of 2 pineapples, * ch 3, in next ch-5 loop make dc, picot and dc. Repeat from * to tip of pineapple, ch 3, (in center sp of next shell make dc, picot, dc and ch 3) twice. Continue on other side of pineapple, ending with ch 3, sc in next ch-3 sp between pineapples. Work in this manner all around. Join and break off. **2nd rnd:** Skip first picot made on last rnd, attach thread to next ch-3 sp, ch 6, picot, dc in same sp, * (ch 5, in next loop between picots make dc, picot and dc) 9 times; skip first picot of next pineapple, in next sp make dc, picot and dc. Repeat from * around. Join and break off.

PLACE DOILY . . . Starting at center, ch 8. Join. **1st to 5th rnds incl:** Repeat 1st to 5th rnds incl of Centerpiece. **6th rnd:** Repeat 5th rnd once more. **7th rnd:** Ch 3, 5 dc in first loop, 6 dc in each loop around. **8th and 9th rnds:** Repeat 11th and 12th rnds of Centerpiece (28 loops on 8th rnd). **10th and 11th rnds:** Repeat 13th and 15th rnds of Centerpiece. **12th to 15th rnds incl:** Work in established pattern, having 2 additional sts on chains between dc's on every other rnd. **16th to 19th rnds incl:** Repeat 22nd to 25th rnds incl of Centerpiece. Complete pineapples individually and make edging exactly as for Centerpiece.

GLASS DOILY . . . Starting at center, ch 8. Join. **1st and 2nd rnds:** Repeat 1st and 2nd rnds of Centerpiece. **3rd rnd:** Repeat 12th rnd of Centerpiece. **4th rnd:** Ch 6, picot, dc in next dc, * ch 3, dc in next dc, picot, dc in next dc. Repeat from * around. Join. **5th rnd:** Sl st to center of next ch-3, ch 6, picot, dc in base of ch-6, * ch 5, in center st of next ch-3 make dc, picot and dc. Repeat from * around. Join. **6th to 9th rnds incl:** Repeat 22nd to 25th rnds incl of Centerpiece. Complete exactly as for Place Doily. 🍍

Pineapple Frosting Place Settings

Materials Required — AMERICAN THREAD COM-PANY "STAR" MERCERIZED CROCHET COTTON, Article 20, Size 30.

5—325 yd. Balls White, Ecru, or Cream for set of 5 Doilies.

Steel Crochet Hook No. 12.

Doily measures about 14 inches.

Ch 8, join to form a ring, ch 4, work 23 tr c in ring, join in 4th st of ch.

2nd Row. Ch 5, skip 1 tr c, s c in next tr c, repeat from beginning 10 times, ch 2, d c in joining of 1st row. This brings thread in position for next row.

3rd Row. Ch 6, s c in next loop, repeat from beginning 10 times, ch 3, d c in d c.

4th Row. Work a row of 7 ch loops ending row with ch 3, d c in d c.

5th Row. Work a row of 8 ch loops ending row with ch 4, d c in d c.

6th Row. Ch 8, s c in same loop, * ch 8, s c in next loop, ch 8, s c in same loop, repeat from * 10 times, ch 4, d c in d c.

7th Row. Work a row of 8 ch loops ending row with ch 4, d c in d c.

8th Row. Work a row of 8 ch loops ending row with ch 8, s c in d c.

9th Row. Sl st to loop, ch 4, * thread over twice, insert in loop and work off 2 loops twice, repeat from *, thread over and work off all loops at one time, ch 7, 3 cluster sts with ch 7 between in same loop, (cluster st: * thread over twice, insert in loop and work off 2 loops twice, repeat from * twice, thread over and work off all loops at one time) * ch 2, s c in next loop, ch 2, 3 cluster sts with ch 7 between each cluster st in next loop, repeat from * all around ending row with ch 2, s c in next loop, ch 2, join in 1st cluster st.

10th Row. * 7 s c over next loop, ch 4, 7 s c over next loop, s c in next loop, ch 4, s c in next loop, repeat from * all around.

11th Row. Sl st to 1st loop, * ch 10, d c in next loop, ch 10, s c in next loop, repeat from * 10 times, ch 10, d c in next loop, ch 5, tr c in sl st.

12th Row. Ch 1, s c, ch 3, s c in same loop, * ch 12, s c, ch 3, s c in next loop, repeat from * all around ending row with ch 5, tr c in ch 1.

13th, 14th and 15th Rows. Ch 1, s c, ch 3, s c in same loop, * ch 13, s c, ch 3, s c in next large loop, repeat from * all around ending row with ch 5, tr c in ch 1.

16th Row. Ch 7, d c in same loop, * ch 6, s c in ch 3 loop, ch 6, 2 d c with ch 5 between in next loop, (shell), repeat from * all around ending row with ch 6, s c in ch 3 loop, ch 6, join in 3rd st of ch 7.

17th Row. Ch 5, 9 tr c with ch 1 between each tr c in same shell, ch 6, 2 cluster sts with ch 5 between in next shell. (cluster st: thread over, insert in loop, pull through and work off 2 loops, thread over, insert in same loop, pull through and work off 2 loops, thread over and work off all loops at one time), * ch 6, 10 tr c with ch 1 between each tr c in next shell, ch 6, 2 cluster sts with ch 5 between in next shell, repeat from * all around ending row with ch 6, join in 4th st of ch.

18th Row. Sl st to ch 1 loop, * ch 3, s c in next ch 1 loop, repeat from * 7 times, ch 6, 2 cluster sts with ch 5 between in center of shell, ch 6, s c in next ch 1 loop,

then repeat from 1st * 10 times, * ch 3, s c in next ch 1 loop, repeat from * 7 times, ch 6, 2 cluster sts with ch 5 between in next shell, ch 6, s c in ch 3 loop of 1st pineapple.

19th Row. * Ch 3, s c in next loop, repeat from * 6 times, ch 6, 2 cluster sts with ch 5 between in next shell, ch 6, s c in next 3 ch loop of next pineapple, repeat from beginning all around.

20th Row. * Ch 3, s c in next loop, repeat from * 5 times, ch 6, 3 cluster sts with ch 3 between each cluster st in next shell, ch 6, s c in next 3 ch loop of next pineapple, repeat from beginning all around.

21st Row. * Ch 3, s c in next loop, repeat from * 4 times, ch 6, 2 cluster sts with ch 3 between in ch 3 loop between next 2 cluster sts, ch 3, 2 cluster sts with ch 3 between in next loop between next 2 cluster sts, ch 6, s c in next 3 ch loop of next pineapple, repeat from beginning all around.

22nd Row. * Ch 3, s c in next loop, repeat from * 3 times, ch 6, 2 cluster sts with ch 3 between in center of shell, ch 3, 2 cluster sts with ch 3 between in next ch 3 loop, ch 3, 2 cluster sts with ch 3 between in center of next shell, ch 6, s c in next 3 ch loop of next pineapple, repeat from beginning all around.

23rd Row. * Ch 3, s c in next loop, repeat from * twice, ch 6, 2 cluster sts with ch 3 between in next shell, * ch 5, 2 cluster sts with ch 3 between in center of next shell, repeat from *, ch 6, s c in next 3 ch loop of next pine-

apple, repeat from beginning all around.

24th Row. * Ch 3, s c in next loop, repeat from * ch 6, 2 cluster sts with ch 3 between in next shell, ch 5, 10 tr c with ch 1 between each tr c in next shell, ch 5, 2 cluster sts with ch 3 between in next shell, ch 6, s c in next ch 3 loop of next pineapple, repeat from beginning all around.

25th Row. Ch 3, s c in next loop, ch 6, 2 cluster sts with ch 3 between in next shell, ch 6, s c in next ch 1 loop, * ch 3, s c in next ch 1 loop, repeat from * 7 times, ch 6, 2 cluster sts with ch 3 between in next shell, ch 6, s c in next ch 3 loop of next pineapple, repeat from beginning 10 times, ch 3, s c in next loop, ch 6, 2 cluster sts with ch 3 between in next shell, ch 6, s c in next 1 ch loop, * ch 3, s c in next 1 ch loop, repeat from * 7 times, ch 6, 2 cluster sts with ch 3 between in next shell.

26th Row. Ch 7, s c in remaining loop of pineapple, ch 7, 2 cluster sts with ch 3 between in next shell, ch 6, s c in next 3 ch loop, * ch 3, s c in next loop, repeat from * 6 times, ch 6, 2 cluster sts with ch 3 between in next shell, repeat from beginning all around.

27th Row. Ch 7, 2 cluster sts with ch 3 between in next shell, ch 6, s c in next ch 3 loop, * ch 3, s c in next loop, repeat from * 5 times, ch 6, 2 cluster sts with ch 3 between in next shell, repeat from beginning all around, ch 1, turn.

28th Row. Sl st to ch 3 loop of shell, shell in same space, ch 6, s c in next ch 3 loop, * ch 3, s c in next ch 3 loop, repeat

from * across pineapple, ch 6, 2 cluster sts with ch 3 between in next shell, ch 1, turn.

Repeat last row until 1 loop remains, ch 1, turn, shell in shell, ch 7, s c in remaining ch 3 loop of pineapple, ch 7, shell in shell, break thread.

Join thread in next shell of next pineapple and complete pineapple same as last pineapple.

Continue in same manner until all pineapples are completed.

Join thread in 7 ch loop between pineapples, * ch 5, s c in side of next shell, repeat from * 5 times, ch 5, s c in center of shell, ch 15, s c in center of next shell, ch 5, s c in side of same shell, * ch 5, s c in side of next shell, repeat from * 4 times, ch 5, s c in next loop between pineapples, then repeat from 1st * all around.

Next Row. Sl st to next loop, ch 3, 2 d c in next loop, ch 7, sl st in 5th st from hook for picot, ch 2, 2 d c in same loop, * ch 2, s c in next loop, ch 2, 2 d c in next loop, ch 7, sl st in 5th st from hook for picot, ch 2, 2 d c in same loop, repeat from *, ch 2, s c in next loop, ch 2, tr c in next loop, * ch 7, sl st in 5th st from hook for picot, ch 2, tr c in same space, repeat from * 6 times, * ch 2, s c in next loop, ch 2, 2 d c in next loop, ch 7, sl st in 5th st from hook for picot, ch 2, 2 d c in same loop, repeat from * twice, ch 2, s c in next loop, ch 5, s c in next loop, ch 2, 2 d c in next loop, ch 7, sl st in 5th st from hook for picot, ch 2, 2 d c in same space, continue in same manner all around, break thread.

Island Paradise Table Runner

Shown in color on the back cover.

MATERIAL REQUIREMENTS AND SIZES

No. 50 Mercerized Crochet Cotton and a No. 12 Steel Crochet Hook		No. 30 Mercerized Crochet Cotton and a No. 10 Steel Crochet Hook		Mercerized Crochet and Knitting Cotton and a No. 8 Steel Crochet Hook	
Doily	Oval	Doily	Oval	Doily	Oval
Size in Inches	10 x 19	Size in Inches	13 x 23	Size in Inches	18 x 34
Approximate No. of Yards	300	Approximate No. of Yards	375	Approximate No. of Yards	555

CENTER SECTION - FIRST PINEAPPLE - 1ST ROW: Ch 5, 2 tr (thread twice around hook for a tr) in 5th ch from hook, ch 2, 3 tr in same st as last tr, ch 2, 3 more tr in same st as last tr.

2ND ROW: Turn, a sl st in each of first 3 tr of last row, a sl st in next (ch 2) loop, ch 4, work (2 tr, ch 2 and 3 tr) in same chain loop as last sl st (this forms first shell), ch 5, skip 3 tr, work a shell of (3 tr, ch 2 and 3 tr) in next (ch 2) loop.

3RD ROW: Turn, work a shell in first shell as follows: a sl st in each of first 3 tr, a sl st in (ch 2) loop, ch 4, (2 tr, ch 2 and 3 tr) in same chain loop as last sl st, ch 3, 4 tr in center st of next (ch 5) loop, ch 3, always working shells in (ch 2) loop of shells below, work a shell of (3 tr, ch 2 and 3 tr) in next shell.

4TH ROW: Turn, a shell in first shell, ch 6, skip chain loop, 2 tr in each of next 4 tr, ch 6, skip chain loop, a shell in next shell.

5TH ROW: Turn, a shell in first shell, skip chain loop, work (ch 6 and 1 sc) in each of next 8 tr, ch 6, a shell in shell.

6TH ROW: Turn, a shell in first shell, skip a chain loop, (ch 6 and 1 sc) in each of 7 chain loops of pineapple, ch 6, skip next chain loop, a shell in shell.

7TH ROW: Turn, a shell in first shell, skip a chain loop, (ch 6 and 1 sc) in each chain loop of pineapple, ch 6, skip next chain loop, a shell in shell.

Repeat last row 4 more times.

12TH ROW: Same as last row but work ch 6, 1 sc in chain loop of pineapple.

13TH ROW: Turn, a shell in first shell, ch 6, 1 sc in sc, ch 6, a shell in shell.

14TH ROW: Turn, a shell in first shell, skip 2 chain loops, 3 tr in next shell, ch 1, turn, a sl st in next shell, ch 1, turn, 3 tr in same shell as last tr; break off.

SECOND PINEAPPLE: Join thread with a sl st in first st of foundation chain of first pineapple, ch 4, work (2 tr, ch 2, 3 tr, ch 2 and 3 tr) in same st as last sl st.

Follow directions for first pineapple from 2nd row to end but do not break off.

1ST ROUND: Ch 1, do not turn, 1 sc in top of last tr made, working along end of rows and always placing sts at corner of shells work (ch 7 and 1 sc) over each of next 13 rows, ch 7, 1 sc in corner of 1st row of next pineapple, (ch 7 and 1 sc) over each of next 13 rows, ch 7, 1 sc in opposite corner of next shell in same row, working along opposite end of rows work (ch 7 and 1 sc) over each of 27 rows, ch 7, a sl st in first sc of round (there are 56 chain loops in round).

2ND ROUND: A sl st in each of next 2 sts of chain, 1 sc in same (ch 7) loop as sl sts, * ch 7, 1 sc in same chain loop as last sc, (ch 7 and 1 sc) in each of next 26 chain loops, ch 7, 1 sc in same chain loop as last sc, (ch 7 and 1 sc) in each of 2 chain loops; repeat from * but end with ch 7, 1 sc in next chain loop, ch 7, a sl st in first sc of round.

3RD ROUND: A sl st in each of 3 sts of chain, 1 sc in same chain loop as sl sts, (ch 8 and 1 sc) in each of next 13 chain loops, do not chain, 1 sc in next chain loop, (ch 8 and 1 sc) in each of 29 chain loops, (do not chain), 1 sc in next chain loop, (ch 8 and 1 sc) in 15 chain loops, ch 8, a sl st in first sc of round.

4TH ROUND: A sl st in each of 4 sts, 1 sc in same chain loop as sl sts, (ch 8 and 1 sc) in 12 chain loops, 1 sc in next chain loop, (ch 8 and 1 sc) in 14 chain loops, 1 sc in same chain loop as last sc, (ch 8 and 1 sc) in 14 chain loops, 1 sc in next chain loop, (ch 8 and 1 sc) in 14 chain loops, ch 8, 1 sc in same chain loop as last sc, ch 8, 1 sc in next chain loop, ch 8, a sl st in first sc of round.

5TH ROUND: A sl st in each of 4 sts, 1 sc in same chain loop as sl sts, * ch 8, 1 sc in next chain loop; repeat from * around, end with ch 8, a sl st in first sc (there are 58 chain loops in round); break off.

6TH ROUND: Skip first 2 chain loops of last round, join thread with an sc in next chain loop, * (2 tr, ch 2 and 2 tr) in next sc, 1 sc in next chain loop; repeat from * around ending with (2 tr, ch 2 and 2 tr) in next sc, a sl st in first sc of round.

7TH ROUND: Slip stitch over to 2nd st of first (ch 2) loop, * skip 2 tr, a shell of (2 tr, ch 2 and 2 tr) in next sc, 1 sc in next (ch 2) loop, (ch 8 and 1 sc) in each of the 16 (ch 2) loops, work (a shell in next sc, 1 sc in next ch 2 loop, ch 6, 5 dc in next ch 2 loop, ch 6, 1 sc in next ch 2 loop) 4 times; repeat from *, a sl st in first tr of round.

8TH ROUND: Sl st over to next (ch 2) loop (from now on work shells as for center pineapples), ch 4, complete first shell, * (ch 8 and 1 sc) in 16 chain loops, ch 8, work (a shell in next shell, ch 6, skip next chain loop, 2 tr in each of next 5 dc, ch 6) 4 times, a shell in next shell; repeat from * but do not work last shell, end with ch 6, a sl st in top of first ch 4 of round.

9TH ROUND: A shell in first shell, * (ch 8 and 1 sc) in 17 chain loops, ch 8, a shell in next shell, skip next chain loop, (ch 6 and 1 sc) in each of 10 tr, ch 6, a shell in next shell, work (skip next chain loop, 'ch 6 and 1 sc' in 10 tr, ch 6, a shell in next shell) 3 more times; repeat from * but end same as last round.

10TH ROUND: A shell in first shell, * (ch 8 and 1 sc) in 18 chain loops, ch 8, a shell in next shell, work (skip next chain loop, 'ch 6 and 1 sc' in 9 chain loops, ch 6, a shell in next shell) 4 times; repeat from * but end same as last round.

11TH ROUND: A shell in first shell, * (ch 8 and 1 sc) in 19 chain loops, ch 8, a shell in shell, work (skip next chain loop, 'ch 6 and 1 sc' in 8 chain loops, ch 6, a shell in shell) 4 times; repeat from * but end same as last round.

12TH ROUND: A shell in first shell, * (ch 8 and 1 sc) in 20 chain loops, ch 8, a shell in next shell, work (skip next chain loop, 'ch 6 and 1 sc' in 7 chain loops, ch 6, a shell in next shell, ch 2, 3 tr in same shell as last tr) 3 times, skip next chain loop, (ch 6 and 1 sc) in 7 chain loops, ch 6, a shell in next shell; repeat from * but end same as before.

13TH ROUND: A shell in first shell, * (ch 8 and 1 sc) in 21 chain loops, ch 8, a shell in next shell, work (skip next chain loop, ch 6 and 1 sc' in 6 chain loops, ch 6, a shell in next ch 2 loop, ch 5, a shell in next ch 2 loop) 3 times, skip next chain loop, (ch 6 and 1 sc) in 6 chain loops, ch 6, a shell in shell; repeat from * but end as before.

14TH ROUND: A shell in first shell, * ch. 6, 1 sc in next chain loop, 7 tr in next sc, 1 sc in next chain loop, work (ch 6, 1 sc in next chain loop, a shell in next sc, 1 sc in next chain loop, ch 6, 1 sc in next chain loop, 7 tr in next sc, 1 sc in next chain loop) 5 times, ch 6, a shell in next shell; work (skip next chain loop, 'ch 6 and 1 sc' in 5 chain loops, ch 6, a shell in shell, ch 3, 7 tr in center st of next chain loop, ch 3, a shell in next shell) 3 times, skip next chain loop, (ch 6 and 1 sc) in 5 chain loops, ch 6, a shell in next shell; repeat from * but end as before.

15TH ROUND: A shell in first shell, * work (skip next chain loop, 'ch 6 and 1 sc' in each of 7 tr, ch 6, a shell in next shell) 6 times, work (skip next chain loop, 'ch 6 and 1 sc' in 4 chain loops, ch 6, a shell in next shell, skip next chain loop, 'ch 6 and 1 sc' in 7 tr, ch 6, a shell in shell) 3 times, skip next chain loop, (ch 6 and 1 sc) in 4 chain loops, ch 6, a shell in next shell; repeat from * but end as before.

16TH ROUND: A shell in first shell, * work (skip a chain loop, 'ch 6 and 1 sc' in each of 6 chain loops of pineapple, ch 6, skip next chain loop, a shell in shell) 6 times, ch 2, 3 more tr in same shell as last tr, work (skip a chain loop, 'ch 6 and 1 sc' in each chain loop of pineapple, ch 6, skip next chain loop, a shell in shell, ch 2, 3 more tr in same shell below) 7 times; repeat from * but end with ch 6, 3 tr in same shell as first shell of round, ch 2, a sl st in top of first ch 4.

17TH ROUND: A shell in first shell, * work (skip next chain loop, 'ch 6 and 1 sc' in 5 chain loops, ch 6, a shell in shell, ch 2, 3 more tr in same shell below) 5 times, work (skip next chain loop, 'ch 6 and 1 sc' in each chain loop of pineapple, ch 6, skip next chain loop, a shell in each of 2 ch 2 loops) 8 times; repeat from * but end with ch 6, a shell in (ch 2) loop, a sl st in top of first ch 4.

FIRST SCALLOP - 1ST ROW: A shell in first shell, skip next chain loop, (ch 6 and 1 sc) in each chain loop of pineapple, ch 6, skip next chain loop, a shell in next (ch 2) loop; do not work over remaining sts.

2ND ROW: Turn, a shell in first shell, skip next chain loop, (ch 6 and 1 sc) in each chain loop of pineapple, ch 6, a shell in shell.

3RD ROW: Same as last row.

4TH AND 5TH ROWS: Same as 12th and 13th rows of center pineapple.

6TH ROW: Turn, a shell in first shell, skip 2 chain loops, a shell in next shell.

7TH ROW: Turn, sl st to (ch 2) loop, 1 sc in same chain loop as last sl st, skip 2 tr, (2 tr, ch 2 and 2 tr) in next tr, 1 sc in next shell; break off.

SECOND SCALLOP - 1ST ROW: Join thread with a sl st in top of end tr of 1st row of scallop just completed, a shell in next (ch 2) loop on the 17th round, skip next chain loop, (ch 6 and 1 sc) in 4 chain loops, ch 6, skip next chain loop, a shell in next (ch 2) loop; do not work over remaining sts.

2ND ROW: Same as 2nd row of first scallop but ending with a sl st in the top st of first ch 4 of 2nd row of next scallop.

Repeat 3rd, 4th, 5th, 6th and 7th rows of first scallop. Work 4 more scallops same as second scallop.

SEVENTH SCALLOP - 1ST ROW: Join thread with a sl st in next (ch 2) loop on last round, ch 4, complete shell, ch 6, skip next chain loop, 1 sc in next chain loop, ch 6, a shell in next shell; do not work over remaining sts.

Repeat 5th, 6th and 7th rows of first scallop; break off.

EIGHTH SCALLOP: Turn, join thread with a sl st in next (ch 2) loop on last round; continue to work same as first scallop. Repeat the 7th and 8th scallops twice; repeat the 7th scallop once more. Continue to work scallops over remaining half of doily same as for first half.

Waikiki Table Runner

Materials: 3 Balls CYNTHIA Mercerized Crochet Cotton, Size 30, White or Ecru. Boye Steel Crochet Hook No. 10 or 11.

44 squares will make a runner approximately 15½ x 40 inches. Each square measures 3½ inches.

SQUARE

Ch 8, join with slip st to form ring.

1st row: Ch 3 (to count as 1 D C), 3 D C in ring, ch 4, * 4 more D C in ring, ch 4, repeat from * twice, join with slip st in 3rd st of ch 3 (4 groups).

2nd row: 1 S C in each D C, 6 S C over each ch 4 of previous row, join with slip st in 1st S C.

3rd row: Slip st to between 2nd and 3rd S C, ch 4 (to count as 1 D C and ch 1), 1 more D C in same place, ch 10, * 1 D C between 2nd and 3rd S C over next group, ch 1, 1 more D C in same place, ch 10, repeat from * twice, join with slip st in 3rd st of ch 4.

4th row: Slip st over to 1st space made by ch 10, 15 S C over ch 10, ch 5, * 15 S C over next ch 10, ch 5, repeat from * twice, do not join.

5th row: Skip the 1st S C, 1 S C in each of next 13 S C, skip the last S C in group, ch 5, 1 S C in ch-5 loop, ch 5, * skip the 1st S C of next group, 1 S C in each of next 13 S C, skip the last S C, ch 5, 1 S C in ch-5 loop, ch 5, repeat from * twice.

6th-8th rows incl.: Work same as previous row, always skipping the 1st and last S C of each group and working 1 more ch-5 loop in each corner; there will be 7 S C remaining in each group and 5 loops between groups at the end of the 8th row.

9th row: * Skip the 1st S C, 1 S C in each of next 5 S C, skip the last S C, ch-5 loop in each of first 2 loops, ch 5, 4 D C in next (corner) loop, ch-5 loop in each of next 2 loops, ch 5, repeat from * 3 times.

10th row: * Skip the 1st S C, 1 S C in each of next 3 S C, skip the last S C, ch-5 loop in each of next 2 loops, ch 5, 4 D C in next loop, ch 5, 4 D C in next loop, ch-5 loop in each of next 2 loops, ch 5, repeat from * 3 times, join with slip st in 1st S C.

11th row: Slip st in 2nd S C, ch 8 (to count as 1 D C and ch 5), 1 S C in 1st loop, ch-5 loop in each of next 2 loops, ch 8, 4 D C in next (corner) loop, ch 8, 1 S C in next loop, ch-5 loop in each of the next 2 loops, ch 5, * 1 D C in 2nd S C of next group, ch-5 loop in each of next 3 loops, ch 8, 4 D C in next corner loop, ch 8, 1 S C in next loop, ch-5 loop in each of next 2 loops, ch 5, repeat from * twice, join with slip st in 3rd st of ch 8.

12th row: Slip st to center of 1st loop, 1 S C in loop, ch-5 loop in each of next 3 loops, ch 5, 1 D C between 2nd and 3rd D C in corner, ch 1, 1 more D C in same place; continue working a ch-5 loop in each loop around row, working each corner same as 1st corner, join with slip st in 1st S C.

13th row: Slip st to center of 1st loop, 1 S C in loop, ch-5 loop in each of the next 3 loops, ch 12 (corner), a ch-5 loop in each loop around row, with ch 12 at each corner, join with slip st in 1st S C and fasten off. This completes one square. Make 43 more squares.

JOINING

Holding 2 squares together (with the right sides facing each other) and using same crochet thread, sew the center sts of 2 corner loops together with 2 over and over stitches, make a running stitch through the ch loops on edge to the center st of the next loop, sew to center st of corresponding loop on other square with 2 over and over stitches, continue joining in same manner the center stitches of each loop to the

(continued on page 48)

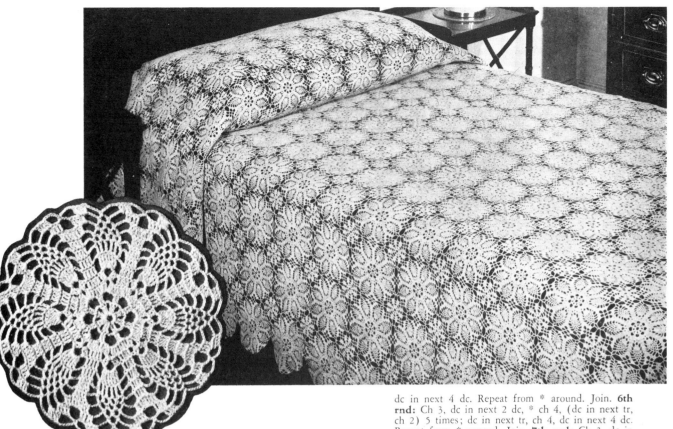

Diamond Head Spread

MATERIALS:

CLARK'S O.N.T. or J. & P. COATS
BEST SIX CORD MERCERIZED CROCHET, size 20:

SINGLE SIZE	DOUBLE SIZE
SMALL BALL:	SMALL BALL:
CLARK'S O.N.T.—141 balls,	CLARK'S O.N.T.—178 balls,
OR	OR
J. & P. COATS —81 balls.	J. & P. COATS —102 balls.
BIG BALL:	BIG BALL:
J. & P. COATS —47 balls.	J. & P. COATS —60 balls.

Steel crochet hook No. 8 or 9.

GAUGE: Each motif measures 4¾ inches in diameter before blocking. For a single size spread about 71 x 104 inches, make 15 x 22 motifs. For a double size spread about 90 x 104 inches, make 19 x 22 motifs.

FIRST MOTIF . . . Starting at center, ch 10. Join. **1st rnd:** Ch 3, dc in ring, * ch 3, 2 dc in ring. Repeat from * 7 times; ch 3, sl st in 3rd st of ch-3. **2nd rnd:** Ch 3, dc in next dc, * ch 5, dc in next 2 dc. Repeat from * around. Join. **3rd rnd:** Ch 3, dc in next dc, * in next sp make 3 dc, ch 2 and 3 dc; dc in next 2 dc. Repeat from * around. **4th rnd:** Ch 3, dc in next 2 dc, * in next sp make 2 dc, ch 5 and 2 dc; skip 2 dc, dc in next 4 dc. Repeat from * around. Join. **5th rnd:** Ch 3, dc in next 2 dc, * ch 3, 6 tr in next sp, ch 3, skip 2 dc,

dc in next 4 dc. Repeat from * around. Join. **6th rnd:** Ch 3, dc in next 2 dc, * ch 4, (dc in next tr, ch 2) 5 times; dc in next tr, ch 4, dc in next 4 dc. Repeat from * around. Join. **7th rnd:** Ch 3, dc in next 2 dc, * ch 5, skip next sp, sc in next sp, (ch 3, sc in next sp) 4 times; ch 5, skip next sp, dc in next 4 dc. Repeat from * around. Join. **8th rnd:** Ch 3, dc in next 2 dc, * ch 6, sc in next ch-3 loop, (ch 3, sc in next loop) 3 times; ch 6, dc in next 4 dc. Repeat from * around. Join. **9th rnd:** Ch 3, dc in next 2 dc, 2 dc in next sp, * ch 6, sc in next loop, (ch 3, sc in next loop) twice; ch 6, 2 dc in sp, dc in next 4 dc, 2 dc in next sp. Repeat from * around. Join. **10th rnd:** Sl st in next 3 dc, ch 3, dc in next dc, 2 dc in next sp, * ch 6, sc in next loop, ch 3, sc in next loop, ch 6, 2 dc in next sp, dc in next 2 dc, ch 4, skip 4 dc, dc in next 2 dc, 2 dc in next sp. Repeat from * around. Join. **11th rnd:** Sl st in next 2 dc, ch 3, dc in next dc, 2 dc in next sp, * ch 6, sc in next loop, ch 6, 2 dc in next sp, dc in next 2 dc, ch 6, sc in next sp, ch 6, skip 2 dc, dc in next 2 dc, 2 dc in next sp. Repeat from * around. Join and fasten off.

SECOND MOTIF . . . Work as for 1st motif to 10th rnd incl. **11th rnd:** Sl st in next 2 dc, ch 3, dc in next dc, 2 dc in next sp, ch 6, sc in next loop, ch 6, 2 dc in next sp, dc in next 2 dc, ch 3, sl st in corresponding sp of 1st motif, ch 3, sc in next sp on 2nd motif, ch 3, sc in corresponding sp on 1st motif, ch 3, dc in next 2 dc on 2nd motif, 2 dc in next sp and complete rnd as for 1st motif (no more joinings).

Make necessary number of motifs, joining adjacent sides as 2nd motif was joined to 1st, leaving 6 sps free between joinings.

FILL-IN-MOTIF . . . Work 1st 2 rnds as for 1st motif. **3rd rnd:** Ch 3, dc in next dc, * dc in next sp, ch 5, dc in same sp, dc in next 2 dc. Repeat from * around. Join. **4th rnd:** Ch 3, dc in next 2 dc, ch 3, sl st in 3rd free sp from joining of motifs, * ch 3, sc in next sp on Fill-in-motif, ch 3, sl st in next sp on large motif, ch 3, dc in next 4 dc on Fill-in-motif, ch 3, tr in next 4 sps on large motif (2 preceding and 2 following joining), ch 3, dc in next 4 dc on Fill-in-motif, ch 3, sl st in next sp on large motif. Repeat from * around. Join. Fill in all sps between joinings in this manner.

Rose and Pineapple Bedspread

Shown in color on the inside back cover.

This bedspread can be made with the following:
The Famous "PURITAN" CROCHET COTTON, Article 40 or "DE LUXE" Quality CROCHET COTTON, Article 346
44 balls White   22 balls Shaded Pinks
Steel crochet hook No. 7 or No. 8
Each motif measures about 8½ inches.
96 motifs 8 x 12 are required for spread measuring about 77 inches x 110 inches.

With Shaded Pinks ch 12, join to form a ring, ch 2 and work 23 s d c in ring (s d c: thread over hook, insert in space, pull loop through, thread over and work off all loops at one time), join in 2nd st of ch, turn.

2nd Row: * Ch 5, skip 3 s d c, sl st in next s d c, repeat from * 5 times (6 loops).

3rd Row: * Ch 1, 1 s c, 2 d c, 6 tr c, 2 d c, 1 s c in next loop, repeat from * 5 times, join.

4th Row: Sl st to 2nd free s d c of 1st row in front of 1st petal, * ch 6, sl st in center free s d c of 1st row in front of next petal, repeat from * 5 times.

5th Row: Ch 1 and work 1 s c, 2 d c, 7 tr c, 2 d c, 1 s c in each loop with ch 1 between petals, join.

6th Row: * Ch 7, sl st in front of work between next 2 petals, repeat from * all around, turn.

7th Row: Same as 5th row, cut thread.

8th Row: Attach White in 1st tr c of any petal, * ch 6, skip 5 tr c, sl st in next tr c of same petal, ch 6, sl st in 1st tr c of next petal, repeat from * all around ending with ch 6, skip 5 tr c, sl st in next tr c, ch 3, d c in same space where thread was attached (this brings thread in position for next row).

9th Row: * Ch 5, sl st in next loop, ch 5, 11 tr c in next loop, ch 5, sl st in next loop, repeat from * 3 times but ending with ch 5, join in d c.

10th Row: Sl st into next loop, ch 3, 1 d c, ch 3, 2 d c in same space, * ch 3, 1 tr c in each of the next 11 tr c with ch 1 between each tr c, ch 3, skip 1 loop, 2 d c, ch 3, 2 d c (shell) in next loop, repeat from * twice, ch 3, 1 tr c in each of the next 11 tr c with ch 1 between each tr c, ch 3, join in 3rd st of ch.

11th Row: Sl st into center of shell, ch 3 (always counts as part of 1st shell), 1 d c, ch 3, 2 d c in same space, ** ch 3, sl st in next loop, * ch 5, sl st in next ch 1 space, repeat from * 9 times, ch 3, sl st in next loop, ch 3, shell in next shell, repeat from ** all around ending to correspond, ch 3, join in 3rd st of ch.

12th Row: Sl st into shell, ch 3, shell in same space, ** ch 3, skip 1 loop, sl st in next loop, * ch 5, sl st in next loop, repeat from * 9 times, ch 3, shell in next shell, repeat from ** all around ending to correspond, join each row.

13th Row: Sl st into shell, ch 3, 1 d c, ch 3, 2 d c in same space, * ch 3, skip 1 loop, sl st in next loop, then work 9 - ch 5 loops across pineapple, ch 3, 2 d c, ch 3, 2 d c, ch 3, 2 d c in next shell, repeat from * all around ending to correspond.

14th Row: Sl st into loop, ch 3, shell in same space, * ch 5, shell in next loop, ch 3, skip 1 loop, sl st in next loop, work 8 - ch 5 loops across pineapple, ch 3, skip 1 loop, shell in next loop, repeat from * all around ending to correspond.

15th Row: Sl st into shell, ch 3, shell in same space, * ch 3, 6 tr c in next loop, ch 3, shell in next shell, ch 3, skip 1 loop, sl st in next loop, work 7 - ch 5 loops across pineapple, ch 3, shell in next shell, repeat from * all around ending to correspond.

16th Row: Sl st into shell, ch 3, shell in same space, * ch 3, 1 tr c in each of the next 6 tr c with ch 1 between each tr c, ch 3, shell in next shell, ch 3, skip 1 loop, sl st in next loop, work 6 - ch 5 loops across pineapple, ch 3, shell in next shell, repeat from * all around ending to correspond.

17th Row: Sl st into shell, ch 3, shell in same space, ** ch 3, sl st in next loop, * ch 5, sl st in next ch 1 space, repeat from * 4 times, ch 5, sl st in next loop, ch 3, shell in next shell, ch 3, skip 1 loop, sl st in next loop, work 5 - ch 5 loops across pineapple, ch 3, shell in next shell, repeat from ** all around ending to correspond.

18th Row: Sl st into shell, ch 3, 1 d c, ch 3, 2 d c, ch 3, 2 d c in same space, * ch 3, skip 1 loop, sl st in next loop, work 5 - ch 5 loops across pineapple, ch 3, 2 d c, ch 3, 2 d c, ch 3, 2 d c in next shell, ch 3, skip 1 loop, sl st in next loop, work 4 - ch 5 loops across next pineapple, ch 3, 2 d c, ch 3, 2 d c, ch 3, 2 d c in next shell, repeat from * all around ending to correspond.

19th Row: Sl st into loop, ch 3, shell in same space, * ch 5, shell in next loop, ch 3, skip 1 loop, sl st in next loop, work 4 - ch 5 loops across next pineapple, ch 3, skip 1 loop, shell in next loop, ch 5, shell in next loop, ch 3, skip 1 loop, sl st in next loop, work 3 - ch 5 loops across next pineapple, ch 3, skip 1 loop, shell in next loop, repeat from * all around ending to correspond.

20th Row: Sl st into shell, ch 3, shell in same space, * ch 5, sl st in next loop, ch 5, shell in next shell, ch 3, skip 1 loop, sl st in next loop, work 3 - ch 5 loops across pineapple, ch 3, shell in next shell, ch 5, sl st in next loop, ch 5, shell in next shell, ch 3, skip 1 loop, sl st in next loop, work 2 - ch 5 loops across next pineapple, ch 3, shell in next shell, repeat from * all around ending to correspond.

21st Row: Sl st into shell, ch 3, shell in same space, * ch 5, sl st in next loop, ch 5, sl st in next loop, ch 5, shell in next shell, ch 3, skip 1 loop, sl st in next loop, work 2 - ch 5 loops across pineapple, ch 3, shell in next shell, ch 5, sl st in next loop, ch 5, sl st in next loop, ch 5, shell in next shell, ch 3, skip 1 loop, sl st in next loop, ch 5, sl st in next loop, ch 3, shell in next shell, repeat from * all around ending to correspond.

22nd Row: Sl st into shell, ch 3, shell in same space, * ch 5, sl st in next loop, ch 5, shell in next loop, ch 5, sl st in next loop, ch 5, 2 d c, ch 3, 2 d c, ch 3, 2 d c in next shell, ch 3, skip 1 loop, sl st in next loop, ch 5, sl st in next loop, ch 3, 2 d c, ch 3, 2 d c, ch 3, 2 d c in next shell, ch 5, sl st in next loop, ch 5, shell in next loop, ch 3, sl st in remaining loop of pineapple, ch 3, shell in next shell, repeat from * all around ending to correspond.

23rd Row: Sl st into shell, ch 3, shell in same space, ** ch 5, sl st in next loop, ch 5, sl st in next loop, ch 5, sl st in center of next shell, * ch 5, sl st in next loop, repeat from * once, ch 5, shell in next loop, ch 3, shell in next loop, ch 3, sl st in remaining loop of pineapple, ch 3, skip 1 loop, shell in next loop, ch 3, shell in next loop, ch 3, sl st in next loop, repeat from * once, ch 5, sl st in center of next shell, * ch 5, sl st in next loop, repeat from * once, ch 5, shell in next shell, shell in next shell, repeat from ** all around ending to correspond.

24th Row: Sl st to center of shell, * ch 5, sl st in next loop, repeat from * 5 times, ch 5, sl st in center of next shell, ch 5, shell in next loop, ch 3, shell in next shell, shell in next shell, ch 3, shell in next loop, ch 5, sl st in center of next shell, * ch 5, sl st in next loop, repeat from * 5 times, * ch 5, sl st in center of next shell, repeat from * once, repeat from 1st * all around ending to correspond, cut thread.

Work a 2nd motif joining it to 1st motif in last row as follows: sl st to center of shell, * ch 5, sl st in next loop,

repeat from * 5 times, ch 5, sl st in center of next shell, ch 5, shell in next loop, ch 3, shell in next shell, shell in next shell, ch 3, shell in next loop, ch 2, join to corresponding loop on side of 1st motif, ch 2, sl st in center of next shell of 2nd motif, * ch 2, join to next loop of 1st motif, ch 2, sl st in next loop of 2nd motif, repeat from * 5 times, * ch 2, join to next loop of 1st motif, ch 2, sl st in center of next shell of 2nd motif, repeat from * once, * ch 2, join to next loop of 1st motif, ch 2, sl st in next loop of 2nd motif, repeat from * 5 times, ch 2, join to next loop of 1st motif, ch 2, sl st in center of next shell of 2nd motif, ch 2, join to next loop of 1st motif, ch 2, shell in next loop of 2nd motif, finish row same as 1st motif, cut thread. Join 3rd motif to 2nd motif and 4th motif to 3rd and 1st motifs in same manner.

JOINING MOTIF: Work 1st 8 rows same as large motif.

9th Row: Sl st to center of loop, ch 3, d c in same space, ch 2, join in joining of 2 large motifs, * ch 2, 2 d c in same space of small motif, ch 2, sl st in center of next shell of large motif, ch 2, 2 d c in next loop of small motif, ch 2, join to next loop of same large motif, ch 2, 2 d c in same space of small motif, ch 2, sl st in center of next shell of same large motif, sl st in center of next shell of large motif (this draws the 2 shells together), ch 2, 2 d c in next loop of small motif, ch 2, sl st in next loop of same large motif, ch 2, 2 d c in same loop of small motif, ch 2, sl st in center of next shell of same large motif, ch 2, 2 d c in next loop of small motif, ch 2, join in joining of large motifs, repeat from * twice, ch 2, 2 d c in same space of small motif, ch 2, sl st in center of next shell of large motif, ch 2, 2 d c in next loop of small motif, ch 2, sl st in next loop of large motif, ch 2, 2 d c in same space of small motif, ch 2, sl st in center of each of the next 2 shells of large motif, ch 2, 2 d c in next loop of small motif, ch 2, join to next loop of large motif, ch 2, 2 d c in same space of small motif, ch 2, join to center of next shell of large motif, ch 2, join in 3rd st of ch, cut thread.

SCALLOP: Attach White in center loop on side of any motif, ch 5, shell in next loop, ch 3, sl st in next loop, * ch 5, sl st in next loop, repeat from * 4 times, ch 3, shell in next loop, ch 5, turn.

2nd Row: Shell in center of shell, ch 3, skip 1 loop, sl st in next loop, * ch 5, sl st in next loop, repeat from * 3 times, ch 3, shell in next shell, ch 5, turn.

3rd Row: Shell in shell, ch 3, skip 1 loop, sl st in next loop, work 3 - ch 5 loops across pineapple, ch 3, shell in next shell, ch 5, turn.

Repeat the last row twice having 1 loop less across pineapple in each row.

6th Row: Shell in 1st shell, ch 3, skip 1 loop, sl st in next loop, ch 3, shell in next shell, ch 5, turn.

7th Row: 2 d c in center of 1st shell, 2 d c in center of next shell, ch 5, skip 1 d c of same shell, sl st in next d c , cut thread, turn.

Next Scallop: Attach White in same center loop of same motif and work 7 rows same as 1st scallop. Work 2 scallops in same manner on side of each motif all around working 4 scallops on corner motifs.

Rose between scallops on outer edge. Work 1st 8 rows same as large motif.

9th Row: Sl st to center of loop, ch 3, d c in same space, count down 7 shells from point of left hand scallop, join in same loop where shell was made, ch 2, 2 d c in same loop of rose, ch 2, sl st in center of next shell on spread, ch 2, 2 d c in next loop on rose, ch 2 ,join to next loop on spread, ch 2, 2 d c in same loop on rose, ch 2, sl st in center of each of the next 2 shells on spread, ch 2, 2 d c in next loop on rose, ch 2, join in next loop on spread, ch 2, 2 d c in same loop on rose, ch 2, join to center of next shell, ch 2, 2 d c in next loop on rose, ch 2, sl st in joining of motifs on spread, ch 2, 2 d c in same loop on rose, ch 2, sl st in center of next shell, ch 2, 2 d c in next loop on rose, ch 2, 2 d c in next loop on spread, ch 2, 2 d c in same loop on rose, ch 2, sl st in center of each of the next 2 shells on spread, ch 2, 2 d c in next loop on rose, ch 2, join in next loop on spread, ch 2, 2 d c in same loop on rose, ch 2, sl st in center of next shell, ch 2, 2 d c in next loop on rose, ch 2, sl st in next loop on spread where scallop shell was made, ch 2, 2 d c in same loop on rose, * ch 3, shell in next loop on rose, repeat from * 4 times, ch 3, join in 3rd st of ch, ch 2, join in 1st free ch 5 loop on right hand side of scallop, ch 3, turn.

Next Row: Working on outside edge of rose sl st in 1st free loop on rose, ch 3, shell in next shell, * ch 3, sl st in next loop, ch 3, shell in next shell, repeat from * 3 times, ch 3, sl st in next loop, ch 2, join in 1st ch 5 loop on side of scallop, cut thread. Work a rose between every 2 scallops at joining of motifs all around.

Pineapple Daiquiri

Chair Back—11 x 16½ inches
Arm Piece—7 x 11 inches

MATERIALS: J. & P. Coats or Clark's O.N.T. Best Six Cord Mercerized Crochet, *Size 30:* **Small Ball:** J & P. Coats—*5 balls of White or Ecru, or 7 balls of any color, or* Clark's O.N.T.—*7 balls of White or Ecru, or 9 balls of any color . . . Steel Crochet Hook No. 10.*

CHAIR BACK . . . Starting at top, ch 245 to measure 18 inches. **1st row:** Dc in 4th ch from hook, dc in next ch, * (ch 3, skip 3 ch, dc in next 3 ch) 3 times; ch 6, skip 6 ch, sc in next 7 ch, ch 6, skip 6 ch, dc in next 3 ch. Repeat from * across, ending with four 3-dc groups. Ch 3, turn. **2nd row:** Skip first dc, dc in next 2 dc, * (ch 3, dc in next 3 dc) 3 times; ch 7, skip 1 sc, sc in next 5 sc, ch 7, dc in next 3 dc. Repeat from * across, ending with dc in last 2 dc, dc in top of turning chain. Ch 3, turn. **3rd row:** Skip first dc, dc in next 2 dc, * (ch 3, dc in next 3 dc) 3 times; ch 8, skip 1 sc, sc in next 3 sc, ch 8, dc in next 3 dc. Repeat from * across, ending as before. Ch 3, turn. **4th row:** Skip first dc, dc in next 2 dc, * (ch 3, dc in next 3 dc) 3 times; ch 9, skip 1 sc, sc in next sc, ch 9, dc in next 3 dc. Repeat from * across, ending as before. Ch 3, turn. **5th row:** Skip first dc, dc in next 2 dc, * (ch 3, dc in next 3 dc) 3 times; ch 6, tr in next ch-9 loop, ch 5, tr in next ch-9 loop, ch 6, dc in next 3 dc. Repeat from * across, ending as before. Ch 3, turn. **6th row:** Skip first dc, dc in next 2 dc, * (ch 3, dc in next 3 dc) 3 times; ch 9, skip next loop, sc in next ch-5

loop, ch 9, dc in next 3 dc. Repeat from * across. Ch 3, turn. **7th row:** Skip first dc, dc in next 2 dc, * (ch 3, dc in next 3 dc) 3 times; ch 8, sc in next loop, sc in next sc, sc in next loop, ch 8, dc in next 3 dc. Repeat from * across. Ch 3, turn. **8th row:** Skip first dc, dc in next 2 dc, * (ch 3, dc in next 3 dc) 3 times; ch 7, sc in next loop, sc in next 3 sc, sc in next loop, ch 7, dc in next 3 dc. Repeat from * across. Ch 3, turn. **9th row:** Skip first dc, dc in next 2 dc, * (ch 3, dc in next 3 dc) 3 times; ch 6, sc in next loop, sc in next 5 sc, sc in next loop, ch 6, dc in next 3 dc. Repeat from * across. Ch 3, turn.

Repeat 2nd to 9th rows incl until piece measures 8 inches, ending with the 4th row. Ch 3, turn.

Now work pineapples individually as follows: **1st row:** Skip first dc, dc in next 2 dc, ch 4, skip next 3 dc, in next sp make 2 dc, ch 5 and 2 dc (shell); ch 4, skip next sp, dc in next 3 dc. Ch 3, turn. **2nd row:** Skip first dc, dc in next 2 dc, ch 4, 11 tr in ch-5 loop of shell, ch 4, dc in next 2 dc, dc in top of turning chain. Ch 3, turn. **3rd row:** Skip first dc, dc in next 2 dc, ch 4, tr in next tr, (ch 1, tr in next tr) 10 times; ch 4, dc in next 2 dc and in top of turning chain. Ch 3, turn. **4th row:** Skip first dc, dc in next 2 dc, ch 4, sc in next ch-1 sp, (ch 3, sc in next ch-1 sp) 9 times; ch 4, dc in next 2 dc, dc in top of turning chain. Ch 3, turn. **5th row:** Skip first dc, dc in next 2 dc, ch 4, sc in next ch-3 loop, (ch 3, sc in next ch-3 loop) 8 times; ch 4, dc in next 2 dc, dc in turning chain. Ch 3, turn. **6th row:** Skip first dc, dc in next 2 dc, ch 4, sc in next ch-3 loop, (ch 3, sc in next ch-3 loop) 7 times; ch 4, dc in next 2 dc, dc in turning chain. Ch 3,

turn. Continue in this manner until only one ch-3 loop remains in center of pineapple. Ch 3, turn. **Next row:** Dc in next 2 dc, ch 4, sc in next ch-3 loop, ch 4, dc in next 2 dc and in turning chain. Ch 3, turn. **Following row:** Dc in next 4 dc, dc in next turning chain. Ch 4, turn. Sl st in turning chain at end of row. Break off.

Attach thread to next dc and work other pineapples to correspond.

BORDER . . . **1st rnd:** Attach thread to end space on starting chain and, working along. long side, make * (ch 7, sc in next sp) 3 times; ch 7, sc in center sc in next sc-group, ch 9, sc in next loop, ch 7, sc in next sp. Repeat from * across to corner, ch 7, sc in corner, ch 7, skip 1 row, sc in next row. Continue in this manner along short side, ending with sc at end of 1st row of first pineapple; ** (ch 7, sc in next row) 13 times; ch 7, sc in next loop, (ch 7, sc in next row) 14 times; 11 sc in next 2 loops, sc in next row. Repeat from ** around pineapples, then finish other short side to correspond. Join. **2nd rnd:** Sl st to center of next loop, * ch 7, sc in next loop. Repeat from * across to corner loop, in corner loop make sc, ch 7 and sc; ** ch 7, sc in next loop. Repeat from ** until ch-7 loops are made around first pineapple; ch 5, sc in next loop of second pineapple, ch 3, sc in adjacent loop of first pineapple, ch 3, sc in next loop on second pineapple. Join next 3 loops as first loop was joined. Then work all other pineapples in the same way and complete other side to correspond. Join and break off.

ARM PIECE (Make 2) . . . Ch 98 to measure 7½ inches. Work exactly as for Chair Back.

Piña Colada

Chair Back—12½ x 17½ inches
Arm Piece—7 x 11 inches

MATERIALS: J. & P. COATS OR CLARK'S O.N.T. BEST SIX CORD MERCERIZED CROCHET, *Size 30:* **Small Ball:** J. & P. COATS—*8 balls of White or Ecru, or 9 balls of any color, or* CLARK'S O.N.T.—*12 balls of White or Ecru, or 14 balls of any color* . . . Steel Crochet Hook No. 10.

CHAIR BACK . . . Make a chain 23 inches long (14 ch sts to 1 inch). **1st row:** In 4th ch from hook make dc, ch 3 and 2 dc; * (ch 5, skip 3 ch, sc in next ch) 5 times; ch 5, skip 3 ch, in next ch make 2 dc, ch 3 and 2 dc (shell). Repeat from * across, ending with a shell (10 shells in row). Cut off remaining chain. Ch 5, turn. **2nd row:** In sp of shell make 2 dc, ch 3 and 2 dc (shell made over shell), * ch 5, skip 1 loop, sc in next loop, (ch 5, sc in next loop) 3 times; ch 5, shell over shell. Repeat from * across, ending with shell over shell. Ch 4, turn. **3rd row:** * 15 tr in sp of next shell, ch 5, skip 1 loop, sc in next loop, (ch 5, sc in next loop) twice; ch 5. Repeat from * across, ending with 15 tr in last shell. Ch 5, turn. **4th row:** Skip first tr, * (tr in next tr, ch 1) 14 times; tr in next tr, ch 5, skip 1 loop, (sc in next loop, ch 5) twice. Repeat from * across, ending with tr. Ch 5, turn. **5th row:** * (Sc in next ch-1 sp, ch 3) 13 times; sc in next ch-1 sp, ch 5, skip 1 loop, sc in next loop, ch 5. Repeat from * across. Ch 5,

turn. **6th row:** * (Sc in ch-3 loop, ch 3) 12 times; sc in next ch-3 loop, ch 3. Repeat from * across. Ch 5, turn. **7th row:** * (Sc in ch-3 loop, ch 3) 11 times; sc in next ch-3 loop, ch 3. Repeat from * across. Ch 5, turn. **8th row:** * (Sc in ch-3 loop, ch 3) 10 times; sc in next ch-3 loop, ch 5. Repeat from * across. Ch 5, turn. **9th row:** * (Sc in ch-3 loop, ch 3) 9 times; sc in next ch-3 loop, ch 5. Repeat from * across. Ch 5, turn. **10th row:** * (Sc in ch-3 loop, ch 3) 8 times; sc in next ch-3 loop, ch 7. Repeat from * across. Ch 5, turn. **11th row:** * (Sc in ch-3 loop, ch 3) 7 times; sc in next ch-3 loop, ch 8. Repeat from * across. Ch 5, turn.

12th row: * (Sc in ch-3 loop, ch 3) 6 times; sc in next ch-3 loop, ch 5, sc in next loop, ch 5. Repeat from * across. Ch 5, turn. **13th row:** * (Sc in ch-3 loop, ch 3) 5 times; sc in next ch-3 loop, ch 5, 2 sc in next loop, sc in next loop, ch 5. Repeat from * across. Ch 5, turn. **14th row:** * (Sc in ch-3 loop, ch 3) 4 times; sc in next ch-3 loop, ch 5, 2 sc in next loop, sc in next 5 sc, 2 sc in next loop, ch 5. Repeat from * across. Ch 5, turn. **15th row:** * (Sc in ch-3 loop, ch 3) 3 times; sc in next ch-3 loop, ch 5, 2 sc in next loop, sc in next 9 sc, 2 sc in next loop, ch 5. Repeat from * across. Ch 5, turn. **16th row:** * (Sc in ch-3 loop, ch 3) twice; sc in next ch-3 loop, ch 5, 2 sc in next loop, sc in next 11, 2 sc in next loop, ch 5. Repeat from * across. Ch 5, turn. **17th row:** * Sc in ch-3 loop, ch 3, sc in next loop, ch 5,

2 sc in next loop, sc in next 2 sc, 2 sc in next loop, ch 5, 2 sc in same loop, sc in next 2 sc, 2 sc in next loop, ch 5. Repeat from * across. Ch 3, turn. **18th row:** * Sc in next ch-3 loop, ch 5, 2 sc in next loop, sc in next 6 sc, 2 sc in next loop, ch 5, 2 sc in same loop, sc in next 6 sc, 2 sc in next loop, ch 5. Repeat from * across. Ch 5, turn. **19th row:** Sc in next loop, * ch 5, skip 2 sc, sc in next 6 sc, ch 5, sc in next loop. Repeat from * across. Ch 3, turn. **20th row:** In first loop make dc, ch 3 and 2 dc; * ch 5, sc in next loop, ch 5, skip 2 sc, sc in next 2 sc, ch 5, 2 sc in next loop, sc in next sc, 2 sc in next loop, ch 5, skip 2 sc, sc in next 2 sc, ch 5, sc in next loop, ch 5, in next loop make 2 dc, ch 3 and 2 dc (shell). Repeat from * across (10 shells in row). Ch 5, turn. **21st row:** * 15 tr in sp of shell, ch 5, skip 1 loop, sc in next loop, ch 5, 2 sc in next loop, sc in next 5 sc, 2 sc in next loop, ch 5. Repeat from * across. Ch 5, turn. **22nd row:** Skip first tr, * (tr in next tr, ch 1) 14 times; tr in next tr, ch 5, skip 2 sc, sc in next 5 sc, ch 5. Repeat from * across. Ch 5, turn. **23rd row:** * (Sc in next ch-1 sp, ch 3) 13 times; sc in next ch-1 sp, ch 5, skip 2 sc, sc in next sc, ch 5. Repeat from * across. Ch 5, turn. Repeat 6th to 23rd rows incl until the 6th row of Pineapples are completed. Break off.

ARM PIECE (Make 2) . . . Make a chain 10 inches long (14 ch sts to 1 inch) and work exactly as for Chair Back (4 shells on 1st row), until 5 rows of Pineapples are completed.

Honolulu Chair Set

Chair Back—13 x 17½ inches
Arm Piece—8¾ x 13 inches

MATERIALS: J. & P. Coats or Clark's O.N.T. Best Six Cord Mercerized Crochet, *Size 30:* **Small Ball:** J. & P. Coats—*10 balls of White or Ecru, or 13 balls of any color, or* Clark's O.N.T.—*16 balls of White or Ecru, or 19 balls of any color . . . Steel Crochet Hook No. 10.*

GAUGE: Each motif measures 4⅜ inches.

CHAIR BACK—First Motif . . . Starting at center, ch 10. Join with sl st to form ring. **1st rnd:** Ch 3, 19 dc in ring. Sl st in top of ch-3. **2nd rnd:** Sc in same place as sl st, * ch 7, skip 2 dc, sc in next 3 dc. Repeat from * around, ending with 2 sc, sl st in first sc. **3rd rnd:** Sl st in next loop, ch 4, 10 tr in same loop, (ch 5, 11 tr in next loop) 3 times; ch 5, sl st in top of ch-4. **4th rnd:** Ch 5, (tr in next tr, ch 1) 9 times; * tr in next tr, ch 5, sc in next ch-5 loop, ch 5, (tr in next tr, ch 1) 10 times. Repeat from * around. Join last ch-5 with sl st to 4th ch of ch-5. **5th rnd:** * Sc in next ch-1 sp, (ch 3, sc in next sp) 9 times; ch 11. Repeat from * around. Join last ch-11 with sl st to first sc. **6th rnd:** Sl st in next ch, sc in same loop, * (ch 3, sc in next loop) 8 times; ch 5, in next ch-11 loop make 2 dc, ch 5 and 2 dc; ch 5, sc in next ch-3 loop. Repeat from * around. Join. **7th rnd:** Sl st in next ch, sc in same loop, * (ch 3, sc in next loop) 7 times; ch 5, dc in next 2 dc, in next sp make 2 dc, ch 5 and 2 dc; dc in next

2 dc, ch 5, sc in next ch-3 loop. Repeat from * around. Join. **8th rnd:** Sl st in next ch, sc in same loop, * (ch 3, sc in next loop) 6 times; ch 5, dc in next 3 dc, ch 5, in next loop make 2 dc, ch 5 and 2 dc; ch 5, skip next dc, dc in next 3 dc, ch 5, sc in next ch-3 loop. Repeat from * around. Join. **9th rnd:** Sl st in next ch, sc in same loop, * (ch 3, sc in next loop) 5 times; ch 5, dc in next 3 dc, ch 5, dc in next 2 dc, in next sp make 2 dc, ch 5 and 2 dc; dc in next 2 dc, ch 5, dc in next 3 dc, ch 5, sc in next ch-3 loop. Repeat from * around. Join. **10th rnd:** Sl st in next ch, sc in same loop, * (ch 3, sc in next loop) 4 times; (ch 5, dc in next 3 dc) twice; ch 5, in next loop make 2 dc, ch 5 and 2 dc; (dc in next 3 dc, ch 5) twice; sc in next ch-3 loop. Repeat from * around. Join. **11th rnd:** Sl st in next ch, sc in same loop, * (ch 3, sc in next loop) 3 times; (ch 5, dc in next 3 dc) twice; ch 5, dc in next 2 dc, in next sp make 2 dc, ch 5 and 2 dc; dc in next 2 dc, (ch 5, dc in next 3 dc) twice; ch 5, sc in next ch-3 loop. Repeat from * around. Join. **12th rnd:** Sl st in next ch, sc in same loop, * (ch 3, sc in next loop) twice; (ch 5, dc in next 3 dc) 3 times; ch 5, in next loop make 2 dc, ch 5 and 2 dc; ch 5, skip next dc, (dc in next 3 dc, ch 5) 3 times; sc in next ch-3 loop. Repeat from * around. Join. **13th rnd:** Sl st in next ch, sc in same loop, * ch 3, sc in next loop, (ch 5, dc in next 3 dc) 3 times; ch 5, dc in next 2 dc, in next loop make 2 dc, ch 5 and 2 dc; dc in next 2 dc, (ch 5, dc in next 3 dc)

3 times; ch 5, sc in next ch-3 loop. Repeat from * around. Join and break off.

SECOND MOTIF . . . Work as for First Motif until 12th rnd is completed. **13th rnd:** Sl st in next loop, ch 3, sc in next loop, (ch 5, dc in next 3 dc) 3 times; ch 5, dc in next 2 dc, 2 dc in next loop, ch 2, sl st in corresponding loop of First Motif, ch 2, 2 dc in same loop as last dc on Second Motif, dc in next 2 dc, (ch 2, sl st in corresponding loop of First Motif, ch 2, dc in next 3 dc on Second Motif) 3 times; ch 2, sl st in next loop of First Motif, ch 2, sc in next ch-3 loop on Second Motif, ch 3, sc in next loop, ch 2, sl st in next loop of First Motif, ch 2, dc in next 3 dc, (ch 2, sl st in corresponding loop of First Motif, ch 2, dc in next 3 dc on Second Motif) twice; ch 2, sl st in corresponding loop of First Motif, ch 2, dc in next 2 dc on Second Motif, 2 dc in next loop, ch 2, sl st in corresponding loop of First Motif, ch 2, and complete as for First Motif (no more joinings).

Make 3 rows of 4 motifs, joining adjacent sides as Second Motif was joined to First Motif. Where four corners meet join third and fourth corners to joining of previous two corners. Work a round of dc along all edges, keeping work flat and making 9 dc in each corner. Join and break off.

ARM PIECE (Make 2) . . . Make 2 rows of 3 motifs and work exactly as for Chair Back.

Pineapple Bib

MATERIALS:

J. & P. COATS or CLARK'S O.N.T.
BEST SIX CORD MERCERIZED CRO-
CHET, *Size 30:* 1 ball of White,
Ecru or any color.

Steel Crochet Hook No. 10 or 11.

1 yard of narrow ribbon.

Starting at neck edge, ch 128 (to measure 10¼ inches). **1st row:** Dc in 8th ch from hook, * ch 2, skip 1 ch, dc in next ch, ch 2, skip 2 ch, dc in next ch. Repeat from * across (49 sps on row). Ch 5, turn. **2nd row:** In 1st sp make 2 dc, ch 2 and 2 dc (shell is made); * ch 2, skip 1 sp, shell in next sp. Repeat from * across (25 shells on row). Ch 5, turn. **3rd row:** Shell in sp of 1st shell, (shell over shell is made); * ch 3, shell over next shell. Repeat from * across. Ch 5, turn. **4th row:** Shell over shell across with ch-4 between shells. Fasten off. **5th row:** Attach thread in sp of 4th shell from end, ch 3, in same place make dc, ch 2 and 2 dc (thus completing shell); * ch 4, shell over shell. Repeat from * across to within last 3 shells. Turn (3 shells decreased at each end). **6th to 11th rows incl:** Sl st in each st across to center of 2nd shell, ch 3 and complete shell as before, * ch 4, shell over shell. Repeat from * across to within last shell. Turn (1 shell decreased at

each end). Fasten off at end of 11th row (7 shells on 11th row). **12th row:** Attach thread in sp of 1st shell on 4th row, ch 5, shell in same place where thread was attached, (ch 5, shell over shell) 8 times; ch 5, in next shell make 2 dc, ch 5 and 2 dc; * (ch 5, shell over shell) twice; ch 5, in next shell make 2 dc, ch 5 and 2 dc. Repeat from * once more; (ch 5, shell over shell) 9 times. Fasten off.

13th row: Attach thread in sp of 4th shell to right of center shell, ch 5, shell over same shell, ch 4, 12 tr in ch-5 sp of next shell, (ch 4, shell over shell) twice; ch 4, 18 tr in ch-5 sp of center shell, (ch 4, shell over shell) twice; ch 4, 12 tr in sp of next shell, ch 4, shell in next shell. Ch 5, turn. **14th row:** Shell over shell, ch 3, tr in each tr with ch-1 between tr's, ch 3, shell over shell, ch 2, shell over shell, ch 3, tr in each tr with ch-1 between tr's, and finish row to correspond with beginning. Ch 5, turn. **15th row:** Shell over shell, ch 3, skip next sp, sc in next sp, (ch 3, sc in next sp) 10 times; ch 3, shell over shell. Ch 5, turn. Complete small pineapple as follows: **16th row:** Shell over shell, ch 3, skip next ch-3, sc in next loop, (ch 3, sc in next loop) 9 times; ch 3, shell over shell. Ch 5, turn. Continue in this manner, making shell over shell and having one ch-3 loop less on

each following row until 1 loop remains. Ch 5, turn. **Next row:** Shell over shell, ch 3, skip next ch-3, sc in loop, ch 3, shell over shell. Ch 5, turn. **Following row:** Shell over shell, dc in sc, 2 dc in sp of next shell, ch 1, sl st in sp of last shell made (thus joining shells), ch 1, 2 dc in same place where last 2 dc were made, ch 5, turn and sl st in joining of shells (pineapple completed). Fasten off. With right side of 1st row of tr's facing, attach thread to next shell (following pineapple just completed), ch 2, sc in adjacent loop of shell on completed pineapple, ch 2, shell in same shell where thread was attached, ch 3, skip next sp, sc in next sp, (ch 3, sc in next sp) 16 times; ch 3, shell over shell. Ch 5, turn. Complete pineapple in same way as 1st pineapple was made. Fasten off. Work 3rd pineapple in same manner, joining adjacent loops as before. Fasten off.

Attach thread in sp of 1st shell on 12th row, ch 5, shell in same sp, * ch 3, sc in next sp (between shells), ch 3, shell in next shell. Repeat from * 6 more times, ch 3, sc in next sp, ch 3, sl st in ch-5 loop preceding next shell. Fasten off. Attach thread to last ch-5 loop on 3rd pineapple, ch 3, sc in next sp (between shells) and work to correspond with side just completed. Pass ribbon through sps at neck edge. ▐

Pineapple Apron and Tea Cozy

MATERIALS:

J. & P. COATS or CLARK'S O.N.T. BEST SIX CORD MERCERIZED CROCHET, *Size 30:*

SMALL BALL:
J. & P. COATS —3 balls of White or Ecru, or 4 balls of any color,
or
CLARK'S O.N.T.—4 balls of White or Ecru, or 5 balls of any color.

BIG BALL:
J. & P. COATS —2 balls of White, Ecru or Cream.

Steel Crochet Hook No. 10 or 11.
1 yard of matching ribbon, 1 inch wide.

BELT . . . Starting at one narrow end, ch 12. **1st row:** In 4th ch from hook, make 2 dc, ch 2 and 2 dc (shell is made), (skip 3 ch, shell in next ch) twice. Ch 3, turn. **2nd row:** Shell in sp of each of next 3 shells (shell over shell is made). Ch 3, turn. Repeat the 2nd row until piece measures 15 inches. Fasten off.

SKIRT . . . Mark with a pin the center turning ch on one side of Belt. **1st row:** Attach thread to loop formed by the 4th turning ch preceding pin mark, sc in same loop, * ch 4, sc in next loop (formed by next turning ch). Repeat from * 7 more times. Ch 3, turn. **2nd row:** * Shell in next sc, ch 4, in next sc make 2 dc, ch 5 and 2 dc; ch 4. Repeat from * across, ending with shell in last sc. Ch 3, turn. **3rd row:** * Shell over shell, ch 4, 13 tr in next ch-5 loop, ch 4. Repeat from * across. Ch 3, turn.

Hereafter "shell over shell" will be referred to as "s.o.s." **4th row:** * S.o.s., ch 4, tr in each tr making ch-1 between tr's, ch 4. Repeat from * across. Ch 3, turn. **5th row:** * S.o.s., ch 4, sc in next ch-1 sp, (ch 3, sc in next ch-1 sp) 11 times; ch 4. Repeat from * across. Ch 3, turn. **6th row:** * S.o.s., ch 4, skip the ch-4, sc in next ch-3 loop, (ch 3, sc in next loop) 10 times; ch 4. Repeat from * across. Ch 3, turn. **7th row:** * In sp of next shell make (2 dc, ch 2) twice and 2 dc, ch 4, sc in next loop, (ch 3, sc in next loop) 9 times; ch 4. Repeat from * across. Ch 3, turn. **8th row:** * Shell in next ch-2 sp, ch 2, shell in next ch-2 sp, ch 4, sc in next loop, (ch 3, sc in next loop) 8 times; ch 4. Repeat from * across. Ch 3, turn. **9th row:** * S.o.s., ch 1, shell in next ch-2 sp, ch 1, s.o.s., ch 4, sc in next loop, (ch 3, sc in next loop) 7 times; ch 4. Repeat from * across. Ch 3, turn. **10th row:** * (S.o.s., ch 2) twice; s.o.s., ch 4, sc in next loop, (ch 3, sc in next loop) 6 times; ch 4. Repeat from * across. Ch 3, turn. **11th row:** * (S.o.s., ch 3) twice; s.o.s., ch 4, sc in next loop, (ch 3, sc in next loop) 5 times; ch 4. Repeat from * across. Ch 3, turn. **12th row:** * S.o.s., ch 5, in next shell make 2 dc, ch 5 and 2 dc; ch 5, s.o.s., ch 4, sc in next loop, (ch 3, sc in next loop) 4 times; ch 4. Repeat from * across. Ch 3, turn. **13th row:** * S.o.s., ch 4, 14 tr in ch-5 sp of next shell, ch 4, s.o.s., ch 4, sc in next loop, (ch 3, sc in next loop) 3 times; ch 4. Repeat from * across. Ch 3, turn. **14th row:** * S.o.s., ch 4, tr in each tr making ch-1 between tr's, ch 4, s.o.s., ch 4, sc in next loop, (ch 3, sc in next loop) twice; ch 4. Repeat from * across. Ch 3, turn.

15th row: * S.o.s., ch 4, sc in next ch-1 sp, (ch 3, sc in next ch-1 sp) 12 times; ch 4, s.o.s., ch 4, sc in next loop, ch 3, sc in next loop, ch 4. Repeat from * across. Ch 3, turn. **16th row:** * S.o.s., ch 4, sc in next loop, (ch 3, sc in next loop) 11 times; ch 4, s.o.s., ch 4, sc in next loop. Ch 4. Repeat from * across. Ch 3, turn. **17th row:** * S.o.s., ch 4, work loops across pineapple, ch 4, s.o.s., ch 2. Repeat from * across. Ch 3, turn. **18th row:** * S.o.s., ch 4, work loops across pineapple, ch 4, s.o.s., ch 1, shell in next ch-2 sp, ch 1. Repeat from * across. Ch 3, turn. **19th row:** * S.o.s., ch 4, work loops across pineapple, ch 4, (s.o.s., ch 2) twice. Repeat from * across. Ch 3, turn. **20th row:** * S.o.s., ch 4, work loops across pineapple, ch 4, (s.o.s., ch 3) twice. Repeat from * across. Ch 3, turn. **21st row:** * S.o.s., ch 4, work loops across pineapple, ch 4, s.o.s., ch 5, in sp of next shell make 2 dc, ch 5 and 2 dc; ch 5. Repeat from * across. Ch 3, turn. **22nd row:** * S.o.s., ch 4, work loops across pineapple, ch 4, s.o.s., ch 4, 15 tr in ch-5 sp of next shell, ch 4. Repeat from * across. Ch 3, turn. **23rd row:** * S.o.s., ch 4, work loops across pine-apple, ch 4, s.o.s., ch 4, tr in each tr making ch-1 between tr's, ch 4. Repeat from * across. Ch 3, turn. **24th row:** * S.o.s., ch 4, work loops across pine-apple, ch 4, s.o.s., ch 4, sc in next ch-1 sp, (ch 3, sc in next ch-1 sp) 13 times; ch 4. Repeat from * across. Ch 3, turn.

25th row: * S.o.s., ch 4, work loops across pineapple, ch 4, s.o.s., ch 4, work loops across pineapple, ch 4. Repeat from * across. Ch 3, turn. **26th row:** * S.o.s., ch 4, sc in next loop, ch 3, sc in next loop, ch 4, s.o.s., ch 4, work loops across pineapple, ch 4. Repeat from * across. Ch 3, turn. **27th row:** * S.o.s., ch 4, sc in next loop, ch 4, s.o.s., ch 4, work loops across pineapple, ch 4. Repeat from * across. Ch 3, turn. **28th row:** * S.o.s., ch 2, s.o.s., ch 4, work loops across pine-apple, ch 4. Repeat from * across. Ch 3, turn. **29th row:** Same as 9th row, making 8 loops over each pineapple. **30th row:** Same as 10th row, making 7 loops over each pineapple. Continue thus in pattern until 1 loop remains at tip of pineapples on 5th pineapple row. **Next row:** * S.o.s., ch 4, work loops across pineapple, ch 4, s.o.s., ch 4, sc in loop, ch 4. Repeat from * across. Ch 3, turn. Now work over pineapples individually as follows: **1st row:** S.o.s., ch 4, work loops across pineapple, ch 4, s.o.s. Ch 3, turn. Repeat this row until 1 loop remains. Ch 3, turn. **Last row:** S.o.s., ch 4, sc in next loop, ch 4, 2 dc in sp of next shell, ch 1, sl st in sp of last complete shell made, ch 1, 2 dc in same place as last 2 dc were made. Fasten off. Attach thread to 1st shell of next pineapple and complete the point in same manner. Continue thus until all points have been worked.

BIB . . . Mark with a pin the center turning ch on other long side of Belt.

1st row: Attach thread to loop formed by 2nd turning ch preceding pinmark, ch 3 and complete shell as before, ch 6, skip next turning ch, in loop formed by next turning ch make 2 dc, ch 5 and 2 dc; ch 6, skip next turning ch, shell in loop formed by next turning ch. Ch 3, turn. **2nd row:** S.o.s., ch 4, 13 tr in ch-5 sp of next shell, ch 4, s.o.s. Ch 3, turn. **3rd to 15th rows incl:** Same as 4th to 16th rows of Skirt disregarding the phrase "Repeat from * across" but ending each row to correspond with beginning. Ch 3, turn. You are now working over two pineapples. **16th to 25th rows incl:** Work as for 17th to 26th rows incl of Skirt having 1 loop less on each row of pineapples and ending with shell in last shell. **Next row:** * S.o.s., ch 4, work loops across pineapple, ch 4, s.o.s., ch 2. Repeat from * across. Ch 3, turn. Now work pineapples individually as before.

EDGING . . . This is worked along outer edges of Bib and Skirt as follows: **1st row:** Attach thread to turning ch preceding 1st shell on 1st row of Bib, shell in 1st loop formed by turning ch on side of Bib, * ch 2, shell in next loop. Repeat from * across 1 point, ch 2, sc in ch 2 between points, ch 2, shell in 1st free loop on next point and continue thus, ending with shell in last free loop of Bib, sl st in next free loop on Belt. Ch 3, turn. **2nd row:** * In sp of shell make dc, p and dc—to make a p, ch 4, sc in 4th ch from hook— ch 3, sc in next ch-2 sp, ch 3. Repeat from * across, ending with sl st where thread was attached. Fasten off. Work two rows of edging all along outer edges of Skirt. Fasten off. Cut ribbon in two ½-yard lengths and sew a piece to each end of belt.

Tea Cozy

MATERIALS:

J. & P. COATS or CLARK'S O.N.T. BEST SIX CORD MERCERIZED CROCHET, *Size 30:*

Small Ball:
J. & P. Coats —4 balls of White or Ecru, or 5 balls of any color,
or
Clark's O.N.T.—5 balls of White or Ecru, or 6 balls of any color.

Big Ball:
J. & P. Coats —2 balls of White, Ecru or Cream.

Steel Crochet Hook No. 10 or 11.

2/3 yard of quilted satin of a contrasting color.

Starting at bottom, make a chain about 18 inches long (11 ch sts to an inch). **1st row:** Dc in 5th ch from hook, dc in next ch, * ch 2, dc in next 2 ch (shell is made), ch 8, skip 9 ch, dc in next 2 ch, ch 5, dc in next 2 ch, ch 8, dc in next 2 ch. Repeat from * across until 11 shells in all are made (6 shells with ch-2 between dc's and 5

shells with ch-5 between dc's). Cut off remaining chain. Ch 3, turn. **2nd row:** In sp of shell make 2 dc, ch 2 and 2 dc (shell over shell is made), * ch 5, 13 tr in ch-5 sp of next shell, ch 5, shell over shell. Repeat from * across. Ch 3, turn.

Hereafter "shell over shell" will be referred to as "s.o.s."

3rd to 26th rows incl: Same as 4th to 27th rows incl of the Skirt of Apron (above). Ch 3, turn. **27th row:** (S.o.s.) twice, ch 4, work loops across pine-apple, ch 4, s.o.s. and continue in pat-tern across, ending with shell in each of last 2 shells. Ch 3, turn. **28th row:** Sl st in 1st shell, shell over next shell, ch 4, work loops across pineapple, ch 4, s.o.s. and continue in pattern across, ending with shell in next to last shell, sl st in last shell. Ch 3, turn. **29th row:** S.o.s., ch 4, work loops across pineapple and continue in pattern across, ending with shell in last shell. Ch 3, turn. Work in established pattern, beginning and ending each row with 1 shell until 1 loop remains on pineapples of 3rd pineapple row. Ch 3, turn. **Next row:**

S.o.s., ch 4, sc in loop, ch 4, s.o.s., and continue in pattern across, ending row to correspond with beginning. Ch 3, turn. **Following 2 rows:** Same as 27th and 28th rows. Work thus in established pattern until 4 rows of loops are worked on pineapples of 6th pineapple row. **Last row:** Work shell over shell and shell in every other loop of pineapples working ch-3 between shells. Fasten off. Work another piece same as this. Place these 2 pieces together and, working over both thicknesses, make an edging of 2 rows as for the Apron (above), all along edges except the 2 bottom edges. Stretch out to shape and press with a damp cloth. Cut 2 pieces of quilted satin to exact measurements of cro-cheted piece including edging. Sew these 2 pieces together, leaving bottom edges free. Cut 2 other pieces of quilted satin, slightly less than measurements of crocheted piece and sew together as before. Place the smaller pieces inside the larger pieces, having wrong sides face, and sew neatly along bottom edges. Slip crocheted cover over cozy.

Golden Pineapples (continued from page 15)

loop, ch 3, sl st in top of last s c for picot, 2 s c in same loop, ch 5, skip 1 loop, 9 tr c in next loop, ch 5, skip 1 loop, 3 s c, picot, 2 s c in next loop, ch 5, skip 1 loop, 3 d c, ch 3, 3 d c (shell) in next loop, repeat from ° once, ch 5, skip 1 loop, 3 s c, picot, 2 s c in next loop, ch 5, 9 tr c in next picot, ° ch 5, skip 1 loop, 3 s c, picot, 2 s c in next loop, ch 5, skip 1 loop, shell in next loop, ch 5, skip 1 loop, 3 s c, picot, 2 s c in next loop, ch 5, skip 1 loop, 9 tr c in next loop, repeat from ° once, ch 5, skip 1 loop, 3 s c, picot, 2 s c in next loop, ch 5, shell in next picot, repeat from 1st ° all around ending to correspond, ch 5, join.

16th Round. Sl st to center of shell, ch 3, shell in same space, ° ch 7, 1 tr c in each of the next 9 tr c with ch 2 between each tr c, ch 7, shell in next shell, repeat from ° all around ending to correspond, ch 7, join.

17th Round. Sl st to center of shell, ch 3, shell in same space, °° ch 7, s c between 1st 2 tr c, ° ch 4, s c in next ch 2 loop, repeat from ° 6 times, ch 7, shell in next shell, repeat from °° all around ending to correspond, ch 7, join.

18th Round. Same as 13th round of 1st pineapple section but having ch 7 before and after each pineapple instead of ch 5. Finish each pineapple same as previous pineapple starting at 14th round but always working ch 7 instead of ch 5 before and after each pineapple.

EDGE: Attach Shaded Yellows in 1st d c at top of pineapple, °° ch 3, cluster st in space at top of pineapple between the 2 d c groups, ch 3, sl st in top of cluster st for picot, ch 3, sl st in top of next row, working down side of pineapple, ch 3, sl st in top of next row, ° ch 3, d c in top of next row, ch 4, sl st in 3rd st from hook for picot, ch 1, d c in same space, ch 3, sl st in top of next row, repeat from ° twice, ch 3, sl st in 1st free row on side of next pineapple, ° ch 3, d c in top of next row, ch 4, sl st in 3rd st from hook for picot, ch 1, d c in same space, ch 3, sl st in top of next row, repeat from ° twice, ch 3, sl st in top of next row, repeat from °° all around ending to correspond, join, cut thread.

Pineapple Placemat (continued from page 27)

tr, sc in next tr, ch 10, sc in center of corner ch-9 lp, ** ch 10, sk 2 tr, sc in next tr, ch 10, sc in next ch-11 lp, ch 10, sc in next ch-5 lp. Repeat from * around, join and fasten off. With Shd. Yellows, ch 5, 3 dc in 4th ch from hook, ch 3, sl st in same st, sl st in next (center) st of flower, (ch 4, 3 dc in 4th ch from hook, ch 3, sl st in same st, sl st in center st) 3 times. Fasten off and sew on flower in center of Motif. With Green Floss, make a French Knot in center of flower, wrapping it 5 times around needle.

2d MOTIF—Repeat 9th rnd. to **, ch 5, sl st in 1st lp on one side of 1st Motif, ch 5, sk 2 tr back on 2d Motif, sc in next tr, ch 5, sl st in next lp on 1st Motif, ch 5, sc back in next ch-11 lp on 2d Motif, ch 5, sl st in next lp on 1st Motif, ch 5, sc back in next ch-5 lp on 2d Motif, ch 5, sl st in next lp on 1st Motif, ch 5, sc back in next ch-11 lp on 2d Motif, ch 5, sl st in next lp on 1st Motif, ch 5, sk 2 tr back on 2d Motif, sc in next tr, ch 5, sl st in next lp on 1st Motif, ch 5, sc back in corner lp on 2d Motif. Finish rnd. as for 1st Motif.

Make 4 rows of 6 Motifs (or other desired size), joining adjacent sides as 2d Motif was joined to 1st Motif.

EDGE—Join Green to 1st lp on 1 side of Doily, ** (ch 10, sc in next lp) 5 times, * ch 10, tr in next (corner) sc on same Motif, tr in corner sc on next Motif, (ch 10, sc in next lp) 6 times. Repeat from * across to corner, ch 10, tr in corner sc, ch 10, sc in next lp. Repeat from ** around, join and fasten off.

2d rnd—Join Shd. Yellows to 1st ch-10 lp on 1 side of Doily, ch 1, sc in same place, * ch 1, 5 dc in same lp, ch 1, sc in same lp, ch 2, sc in next lp. Repeat from * around making 4 ch around corners between scallops. Join to 1st sc and fasten off.

Stretch and pin Doily right-side-down in true shape. Steam and press dry thru a cloth.

Waikiki Table Runner (continued from page 38)

corresponding loop on other square. Join all squares in same way, with 11 squares in each of the 4 strips, then work edging around entire runner.

EDGING

Working from right side of runner, attach thread in 3rd loop before a corner loop, 1 S C in loop, ch 5, 4 D C in next loop, ch 5, 1 S C in next loop, ch 5, 1 D C in 3rd st of corner loop, ch 1, 1 more D C in same st, ch 8, skip 6 sts on loop, 1 D C in next st, ch 1, 1 more D C in same st, ch 5, 1 S C in next loop, ch 5, 4 D C in next loop, * ch-5 loop in each of next 4 loops, ch 5, 4 D C in next loop, ch 5, 1 S C in next loop, ch 6, thread over hook 3 times, insert hook in joining st, thread over and through 2 loops 4 times in succession (D Tr), ch 5, another D Tr in the same place, ch 6, 1 S C in next ch-5 loop, ch 5, 4 D C in next loop, repeat from * around entire edge, working each corner in same manner as 1st corner, join with slip st in 1st S C.

2nd row: Slip st to 2nd st of 1st loop, ch 3, 3 D C in same loop, ch 5, 4 D C in next loop, ch 5, 1 S C in next loop, ch 8, 1 D C in center st of corner loop, ch 1, 1 more D C in same st, ch 8, 1 S C in next loop, ch 5, 4 D C in next loop, ch 5, 4 D C in next loop, * ch-5 loop in each of next 3 loops, ch 5, 4 D C in next loop, ch 5, 4 D C in next loop, ch 8, 1 S C in next loop (between D Tr), ch 8, 4 D C in next ch-5 loop, ch 5, 4 D C in next loop, repeat from * around edge, working each corner same as 1st corner, join with slip st in 1st st of ch 3.

3rd row: Slip st in each of next 3 D C and 1st 2 sts of 1st loop, ch 3, 3 D C in same loop, ch 5, 1 S C in next loop, ch 8, 1 S C in next loop, ch 12 (corner), 1 S C in next loop, ch 8, 1 S C in next loop, ch 5, 4 D C in next loop, * ch-5 loop in each of next 4 loops, ch 5, 4 D C in next loop, ch-8 loop in each of next 2 loops, ch 8, 4 D C in next loop, repeat from * around edge, working each corner same as 1st corner, join with slip st in 3rd st of ch 3 and fasten off.